S0-BFD-296

REVERE BEACH ELEGY

Praise for Revere Beach Elegy & Roland Merullo:

"Sentimentality is cheap. Real emotions are difficult to render. Memoirists walk a tightrope between sentimentality and simple feeling. What gives *Revere Beach Elegy* its vitality and 'worth' is the author's taut prose and his fearlessness to run across that tightrope."
- Greg Lalas, *Boston Magazine*

"Merullo writes about [the adventures] and the people and places of his life with careful reflection and painstaking kindness..."
- *Publishers Weekly*

"*Revere Beach Elegy* is an autobiography in ten essays that is sublimely refreshing in its love and generosity. Merullo's prose, as he outlines the worlds he cherishes, has a luminous subtlety that brings alive rich layers of feeling in an immediate intelligible manner. His eye stays intently trained on how we guide ourselves through life."
- Michael Upchurch, *The Seattle Times*

"Merullo has a knack for rendering emotional complexities, paradoxes, or impasses in a mere turn of the phrase."
- *Chicago Tribune*

"[Merullo's] gift is slipping gentle spiritual lessons into easy-reading narratives...with effortless charm."
- *The Christian Science Monitor*

Also by Roland Merullo

Fiction

Leaving Losapas
A Russian Requiem
Revere Beach Boulevard
In Revere, In Those Days
A Little Love Story
Golfing with God
Breakfast with Buddha
American Savior
Fidel's Last Days
The Talk-Funny Girl

Non Fiction

Passion for Golf
Revere Beach Elegy
The Italian Summer: Golf, Food and Family at Lake Como
Demons of the Blank Page

REVERE BEACH ELEGY

A Memoir of Home and Beyond

Roland Merullo

AJAR Contemporaries

AJAR Contemporaries
publisher@pfppublishing.com
OR c/o
PFP, Inc
144 Tenney Street
Georgetown, MA 01833

AJAR Contemporaries Edition, January 2011

© 2002 Roland Merullo
All Rights Reserved

Printed in the United States of America

"What a Father Leaves" was first published in *Witness* magazine, American Families issue. "Summer School" was first published in *Forbes FYI* magazine. "My Two Heavens" and "The Notion of North" were first published in *The Boston Sunday Globe Magazine*, copyright Globe Newspaper Company, all rights reserved, used by permission. "Third Rate Romance" by Russell Smith © 1974 Fourth Floor Music, Inc (ASCAP). All rights administered by WB Music Corp. (ASCAP). All rights reserved. Used by permission.

Cover Art: Amanda Merullo

Library of Congress Cataloging-in-Publication Data
Merullo, Roland
Revere Beach Elegy: A Memoir of Home and Beyond/Roland Merullo
First AJAR Contemporaries edition © 2011
ISBN-10 0-9833139-1-1
ISBN-13 9780983313915
Reprint. Previously published: Boston: Beacon Press 2002

For Alexandra and Juliana

and in memory of Lois Haydock

All I mark as my own, you shall offset it with your own,

Else it were time lost listening to me.

Walt Whitman

CONTENTS

What a Father Leaves

On a June day when the world was at war, my father came into this life in a simple wooden house on Tapley Avenue, in Revere, Massachusetts. He died, without providing any advance notice, in a slightly fancier home on Essex Street. A little more than sixty-six years separated that birth and that death, a little more than a mile separated those two houses. Though he was an ordinary man in many respects, he knew extraordinary sorrow at an early age, and, later, extraordinary triumph, and among the tempers and memories he bequeathed me was the conviction that it is possible to find a solid bottom beneath those tidal sweeps of good and bad fortune.

His childhood was typical of the childhood of millions of first-generation European immigrants in the first quarter of the twentieth century; he was a small piece of a large family that was caught between the strictures of the old world and the promises and possibilities of the new His parents—Giuseppe Merullo, a tailor, and Eleonora De-Marco Merullo, a housewife—had come to America from poor hilltop villages in southern Italy, settled briefly in Boston's North End, then married and moved a few miles north to the city of Revere—the countryside then—where they bought a house and began to fill it with children. My father was born in 1916, after Philomena and Carmen, and before Gloria, Violet, Anthony, Joseph, and Robert, but no tangible proof of his existence has come down to me from those years, no snapshots of him as a boy, no school papers or early artwork, only scraps of anecdote passed along by his brothers and sisters, who remain close to each other and to me.

His family was, by turns, relatively wealthy and relatively poor. Giuseppe—Joe, as he came to be called—owned his own tailor shop and lost it in a fire, owned one of the first automobiles in the neighborhood and lost it to medical bills after a fall, owned the house on Tapley Avenue, lost it in the Depression, then bought it back again in 1938. At one point in the 1930s, Eleonora had to sell her wedding ring to buy food, and the nearest tailoring work Joe could find was in Rockland, Maine, a twelve-hour drive to the north, in a car with no heater.

The streets were dirt, street lamps shone beneath crimped metal hats the color of poorly cared-for teeth. The Merullo children slept two to a bed, kept warm in winter by bricks that were heated in the coal stove, then wrapped in a towel and placed beneath the blankets at their feet. The family put up their own vegetables and made their own wine and root beer. The boys tilled the garden, shoveled snow, smoked cigarette butts they found on the sidewalk; and the girls listened to opera with their father on Sunday afternoons, cared for the babies, learned to cook at their mother's shoulder, were courted by boys from similar families on chaperoned outings.

The Revere of those days consisted of clusters of plain wooden houses set among rolling fields, its politics controlled by men of English and then Irish descent, its underworld run mainly by Jews, its three-mile crescent shoreline (America's first public beach) fronted by amusement rides, food stands, and dance halls that drew tourists from as far away as the West Coast, its social life revolving around a synagogue and a dozen churches, men's clubs, the Revere Theater on Broadway. Six square miles of salt marsh and low hills a stone's throw from the metropolis, home to Italians, Poles, Russians, French Canadians, Irish, English, Jews, Scots, Germans, and a handful of blacks, the city was unfortunately and perhaps unfairly—known primarily for political scandal, underworld dens, and racetracks. In fact, though, it was not much different from places like Brooklyn, Jersey City, and South Philadelphia: a certain rough humility, an emphasis on family loyalty and the vibrant, sometimes violent, life of the street, a brew of American ambition and European tradition that would, in future generations, bubble over into something more sedate and suburban, leaving room for different immigrants, new dramas.

It was in that hothouse of hope and defeat that the seed of my father's life sprouted. I know that he was a good, perhaps even a brilliant student, that as a young boy he cared so much about his clothes that he would take out his handkerchief and spread it carefully beneath him before sitting down on a neighbor's concrete wall, that he was baptized Orlando and went to school Roland, that he spoke Italian before speaking English but carried no trace of accent into adulthood. Those are the few puzzle pieces that survive. The remainder of his first eighteen years is a wash of American history almost identical to the history of twenty million other Orlandos, Patricks, and Sauls.

My father belonged to the generation of Americans we are now in the process of forgetting, a generation that had the misfortune to make the leap from high school into adulthood with the chasm of a world Depression yawning beneath their boots. In 1934, he graduated from Revere High School with honors, but there was no tradition of college in his family (his older brother and sister had dropped out of high school to help bolster the family income), no money for tuition, no clearly marked route along which his ambition might travel.

In the farms that spread across western Revere then, he found work with a produce company called Suffolk Farms, picking carrots and cucumbers for twelve dollars a week. Over the course of the next few years, he moved up to a public relations position, studied civil engineering in night school, and when he'd earned his certificate, left Suffolk Farms for a job on a surveying crew. "On hot days," he would tell me forty years later, "I couldn't stand to be out there in my clean clothes while the other guys were sweating with their picks and shovels. Some days I took off my shirt and climbed down in the ditches with them and helped them out for a few hours."

That remark speaks volumes about him, about the confusion of longing for better and loyalty to his roots that runs like a refrain through his life. Even after he'd abandoned pick and shovel and surveyor's transit and climbed up into the high, fragile branches of Massachusetts State Government, he could not bring, himself to leave Revere. He still met his childhood friends at Wonderland Dog Track one or two nights a week for an evening of modest losing, still seemed to feel as comfortable lunching with judges and senators at Dini's in Boston as he did with city workers, plumbers, and bookmakers at Louie's corner coffee shop a few blocks from where he'd been born.

The remark speaks to something else, as well. My father was a gregarious man, and cared—sometimes to a fault—what impression he made in society. Like many Italian-American men, many men of all ethnic groups and races, he was shadowed by a societal definition of masculinity that has more to do with being brawny and tough than with any of the finer attributes. He worried that his arms and hands did not look strong enough, he worried about how he had dealt with and would deal with pain. Surrounded by war veterans, star athletes, and street fighters, he was pricked by a nagging devil of doubt because he was none of those things.

I am taking liberties here. He never said any of this to

me. Such tender introspection would have been as alien to him as corned beef to his mother's kitchen. And yet, I have a storehouse of small clues that stand in for his words. I see the footprints of that same devil on the carpet of my own home. I see the strength to be taken from traditional masculine stereotypes, as well as the wreckage they wreak in me, in brothers and cousins, in friends' marriages. Once in a while, in the midst of a discussion of the roles women have been made to play in our society, I hear an echo of my father's voice: "Sometimes on hot days—"

In 1940, he married, and began working as a draftsman for a Boston firm called Stone and Webster, his first real office job. The work consisted of designing power stations and submarine periscopes, and he liked it well enough. The following December, when America was pulled into the war, he tried three times to enlist, but was turned down because of a punctured eardrum, forced to watch as the world convulsed and bled and the men of his generation went off to face their appointed sufferings.

For someone who felt embarrassed about working in a shirt and shoes next to bare-chested men with shovels, the idea of being left behind while neighbors went to war must have been next to unbearable for him. But, other than to state the facts of his case—the punctured eardrum, the three rejections—he did not speak to me about it.

As fate would have it, his own sufferings found him soon enough: on March 26, 1942, his wife of thirteen months died in childbirth. Again, only small pieces of this woman's life have drifted down to me through the shifting seas of familial memory. In the few snapshots I have seen, she is a happy girlfriend and then a happy newlywed, thin, dark-haired, pretty. I know that she was waked in her wedding gown that, in the weeks and months after her death, my father's suffering seemed bottomless. "We would just be sitting down to dinner," one of my uncles told me only a year ago, "and the phone would ring. It would be the caretaker at the cemetery in West Roxbury, where Vi was buried, asking us to send someone over there right away because Roland was sitting next to the grave, weeping, and the caretaker wanted to close up and go home."

But the sense of this grief has reached me only third-hand, and only years after my father's death. Though I often wish it had been otherwise, he did not talk about grief and tragedy with me and my brothers. Every once in a while, during some poignant pause in the busyness of his life, he would be alone with one of us and make a comment like: "Someday I'll tell you everything. Someday we'll sit down and I'll tell you things." But what these things were we had little idea, and the promised "someday" never arrived.

Perhaps in deference to his second wife, my, mother, he never spoke about his first marriage in our presence. I learned of it by a chance remark. Playing in the backyard one summer afternoon, I was summoned to the fence by our elderly neighbor, Rafaelo Losco, who handed over an armful of greens for me to pass on to my grandmother. Rafaelo had another man with him, a visiting brother or friend, and the man was running his eyes over my face with such intensity I felt as though a blind person were fingering my eye sockets and lips. "What is your name?" he demanded.

"Roland."

"Roland's son?"

"Yes."

"I've known your father forty years. I knew his wife when she was growing up. His first wife, I mean."

I only nodded, and turned away with my armful of escarole, but the words claimed a place in my memory. His *first* wife. I was old enough by then—seven or eight—to know something about secrets, to sense that this piece of information had been kept out of my reach for a reason, and I did not mention it, not to my parents or grandparents or brothers or friends, for close to two decades.

It seems peculiar now, that in all the times I must have been alone with my father during those years, I never asked about his first wife, or even let him know that I knew of her existence. It seems strange that he and my mother, and their parents and brothers and sisters, conspired in such a silence when it would have been so much easier all around to tell the story, once, answer the questions, and be done with it.

But ours was a Catholic world in which marriage was supposed to last for all eternity, and this was the 1950s and 1960s, when the ethos of emotional confession had not yet broken the polished shell in which we lived. And I believe there was an element of superstition involved as well, remnant vapors of an ancient stew of belief and mystery: to speak of tragedy would be to invite it. The closest any relative ever came to raising the subject was when one of my father's sisters asked me, in private, what I thought happened when people who'd been married more than once died and went to heaven. Which spouse were they in heaven with, did I have an opinion? Had I heard anything about this at Sunday school?

Whatever the reason or combination of reasons, the fact of my father's first marriage lay in the deep, undisturbed shadows of our family consciousness until the winter of 1978. In that year, I began knocking down, piece by piece and without spite, the edifice of expectations my parents had been erecting since my birth. I'd taken my college degrees a few years earlier, and, after a stint with USIA in the Soviet Union, I'd turned away from both an academic and a diplomatic career. With much fanfare, I joined the Peace Corps, went off to a primitive island in the Pacific, then quit after less than six months. Penniless, long-haired, hosting a menagerie of tropical bacteria, I returned to America and found work driving a cab in Boston, a job which seemed to crush the last of my parents' hope for me like crystal beneath a greasy work boot. In the space of eighteen months, I had gone from being a source of pride to a source of embarrassment, and in December I put the finishing touches on that swan dive into dishonor by announcing that I was moving in with my Protestant girlfriend.

As a boy, I'd seen a neighbor burst into tears at her daughter's engagement to *il protestante*, but it was 1978 now, and such "mixed" marriages no longer shocked Revere's papists. My parents had met Amanda before my

Peace Corps venture, and approved of her from the start. The problem was not Amanda's religion or nationality (my mother, though Catholic, was of English ancestry, so that could hardly be an issue) or even the fact that we were having unblessed sex. The problem was that, by moving in together, we were openly confessing to this unblessed union, making it public, running up the flag of *disgrazia* for everyone in the family, in Revere, to see.

There were harsh words that night in the house on Essex Street, hurt feelings on both sides. My father, mother, and I shouted at each other across a widening chasm, tore at the sticky filaments that bound us, took turns pacing the kitchen, accusing. It had a different feeling than other arguments, the words were sharper, the consequences heavier. I was trying to embarrass them, smudge their good name. They were trying to meddle with my happiness. After that night, my mother stayed angry at Amanda and me for several weeks.

My father was quicker to rebound. After we'd simmered for an hour in separate rooms, I said I was going to take the subway into Boston and spend the night with Amanda, but he offered to drive me, instead.

We left the house in silence, drove along Revere's dark streets, acting out our epic of stubbornness. It did not occur to me that he might have offered the ride out of anything other than his reflexive generosity, a trait I took almost completely for granted at that point. In our culture, stinginess—with money, time, or assistance—was second only to disloyalty on the tablet of cardinal sins: why wouldn't he offer to drive into Boston and back at ten o'clock on a Sunday night?

Somewhere in Chelsea he said: "I guess things don't stand still. I changed my mind on Vietnam. I guess I'll end up changing my mind on this."

I said nothing, determined to win, for once, as I had seen him win so many times. We were climbing the flat arc of the Mystic River Bridge, a cold darkness beyond the windshield, harsh words still echoing behind us.

"You know this will lead to marriage," he went on, and I told him that if this led to marriage, it would be fine with me. He gave one of his short, tight-lipped nods. "She's a nice girl, a family girl."

This high compliment changed the air between us, and it began to seem to me that something positive had come of our fight. We had somehow knocked a hole in the too-respectful shield I'd put up around him, in the notion of father-as-king that brings so much stability to Italian families even as it nourishes the seeds of inadequacy in some sons and grandiose imitation in others. The trick was to thrust aside that notion without trampling on the man behind it, and we had somehow managed that. So I ventured a step into uncharted territory.

"You were married before, weren't you, Pa?"

"That's right."

"What happened?"

"She died."

"How?"

"In childbirth."

For a moment I turned my eyes away, touched, embarrassed, by the grief in his words, thirty-six years after the fact. It seemed to me then that, in two short sentences, I had an explanation for everything: his temper and frustrations, his fear that any telephone call might bring the worst imaginable news, his penchant—almost an obsession—for attending wakes and soothing the bereaved, his armor and distance and pride and stoicism, his superb, sometimes dark, sense of humor, his faith that the universe was ordered beyond any human understanding.

I had a key to him, at last. In love myself, the idea of losing a beloved struck me in a deeper place than it would have on some other night.

I was watching him now across the front seat, but he would not look at me.

"What happened to the baby?"

"The baby died, too."

"And then what was your life like?"

"Bitter," he said. "Until I met your mother. Bitter."

With that word, we buried the subject and never raised it again. In time, relatives would help me fill in some of the details: After Vi's death, my father withdrew almost totally from the social whirl on which he'd thrived. For years and years he did not date. His easygoing personality hardened a bit. He sought solace in his church, his brothers and sisters, a small group of family friends. His parents sold the house on Tapley Avenue (he and Vi had lived in the downstairs apartment) and moved a mile west to Essex Street, and my father passed most of the 1940s that way, enveloped in a womb of sorrow, loneliness, and defeat, while around him the world was again at war.

Very, very gradually he emerged. With the assistance of my mother (a lovely physical therapist who spent two years at Walter Reed Hospital, rehabilitating men who'd lost arms and legs in the war, and then volunteered to work with polio victims at the height of the epidemic—in short, a woman who'd had some experience bringing a bit of light into the lives of the wounded and lonely) his bitterness faded enough for him to want to make another try at building a family.

In 1949, he and my mother were engaged. He went into local politics and was elected to the city council, ran for state representative two years later and was narrowly defeated. On Veterans Day weekend in 1951, Roland Alfred Merullo and Eileen Frances Haydock were wed, and, after a brief honeymoon in Washington, D.C., they moved into the four-room apartment above my father's parents.

In 1952, my mother suffered a miscarriage in her fourth month of pregnancy. In 1953, she bore Roland, Jr., the first of three sons. In 1954, with my mother and me waiting in the car, my father, who had been out of work for the past several weeks, walked into the offices of the Volpe Construction Company in Malden, without an appointment, and asked the boss for a job. The boss, John Volpe, future Governor of Massachusetts, Secretary of Transportation in the Reagan administration, and Ambassador to Italy, gave him a job, not as an engineer but as a worker in the gubernatorial campaign of a man named Christian Herter.

There began an unlikely association that would radically change the course of my father's life. Herter was tall, lanky, and wealthy, and displayed in his speech, clothing, and posture all the entitlements and credentials of what would later come to be known as the White Anglo-Saxon Male Power Establishment. And my father was a big-chested, six-foot Italian who had never spent a week outside his neighborhood, who had not been to college, or to Europe, or even to Vermont, for that matter; a Republican in a nest of Democrats; white and male but entitled to nothing and wanting everything.

They became fast friends, and their friendship endured until Herter's death in 1964. A strong orator, very careful about his clothes and manners, my father was a natural on the campaign trail, a great asset in the predominantly Italian-American precincts north of Boston. When Herter was elected Governor of Massachusetts in 1954, he chose as his personnel secretary a working-class Republican from a provincial neighborhood on Boston's tattered northern cuff.

In any government, but especially in one as patronage fueled as the State Government of Massachusetts, personnel secretary is a position of vastly underestimated power. Acting by the rules on which he had been raised, my father found work for a long list of relatives and friends, filling the agencies of state with men and women he knew and trusted, or simply men and women who needed a boost in their lives, a steady paycheck, a safe niche they could cling to until retirement age. In so doing, he accumulated a huge bank account of favors, an account he would draw on unashamedly later in life, finding summer work for nieces and nephews and sons, interceding with judges, lawyers, cops, making a phone call here, pulling a string there, tweaking and twisting and cajoling and sometimes shoving the many-limbed beast of state power.

At some point in my early twenties, I turned my back on that side of him, refused any further assistance for myself, cast a harsh eye on what seemed to me then little more than nepotism. We used to argue about it from time to time. When I interviewed for my first government job in the USSR, he half-seriously offered to pull some strings for me in Washington. "You do that," I said, "and I'll refuse the job if I get it."

"You don't think other people will be doing that for their own?"

"I don't care," I said, and I didn't. But how easy it was for me, with my fancy education, to cast a righteous and condescending eye upon his string-pulling, the survival by-connection ethos in which and by which the people of his time and place lived. And how clear it is to me now that solitary achievement is not the only measure of worth, that all of us are constantly engaged in a give-and-take of affection and advantage, doing favors and having favors done for us. But I was headstrong then, and full of myself, and, like many other twenty-four-year-olds, planning to remake the world according to my pure vision.

In 1956, Chris Herter went to Washington as Undersecretary of State (in 1958, when Dulles resigned, he advanced to the Secretary's job) in the Eisenhower administration, and offered to bring his personnel secretary along for the ride. But, for my father, Washington was too far from Revere, from his brothers, sisters, and parents, from the faces and corridors he knew. He respectfully declined the offer and seemed, in later years, untroubled by regret. In 1958, the *Boston Globe* printed a picture of Secretary Herter above a story suggesting he would be the party's nominee for president. My father is standing beside him, gearing up, perhaps, for another campaign, revving up old ambitions, ready to give Washington a shot this time. But Herter was already in a wheelchair by then, stricken with polio and about to cede his front-runner status to Richard Nixon. The rest, as they say, is history.

Before Herter left Massachusetts, he offered my father his choice of several high-level if low-paying jobs in the state bureaucracy, among them, head of the Metropolitan District Commission and Director of the Industrial Accident Board. My mother talked him out of the MDC job, a prestigious, but high-profile position that came under regular attack from one camp or another: press, politicians, populace; he settled in as Director of the IAB.

It was a good job, and another man would have been content there, with a corner office overlooking Boston Common, weekly trips to the western part of Massachusetts to inspect safety conditions at state-insured factories, S. S. Pierce food baskets at Christmastime from the managers of those factories, extended lunch hours during which he'd prowl downtown Boston's bargain clothing stores and buy suits and shirts for his friends and brothers, whether they'd asked him to or not.

For a while, in fact, he was happy at the Industrial Accident Board, and from the late fifties until the mid-sixties his life settled into a tame pattern it had not known before

and would not know again. He was president of St. Anthony's Holy Name, a member of the Knights of Colum-
bus, the ITAM club, the Children's Hospital Association.
On summer weekends, he golfed at public courses with
friends he'd known for forty years. He bowled and bet the
greyhounds and played whist for nickels with his brothers,
made the rounds of his sisters' homes for coffee and pa-
stry on Sunday mornings after church. In the vacant lot
next door to his parents' house, he and my mother built
an eight-room, Colonial-style home, a grand structure by
the standards of our street. They took my brothers and me
on modest summer vacations—three days at Lake Winnipesaukee, a week at a friend's house near the Cape Cod
Canal; they drove us to church on Sunday mornings, to
Little League games.

There were smudges on this idyllic tableau, the ordinary frustrations and dissatisfactions of family life. His
temper, short of fuse and short of duration, could be trig-
gered by something as small as a spilt glass of milk, and
our Sunday dinners were sometimes broken up by need-
less argument. He was not as careful with money as he
might have been: I remember him hunkered down over a
table covered with bills, puffing his pipe, unapproachable.
And he might have traded a few hours of his social life for
a few more hours at home.

But he paid his bills, and visited the sick, and came
home sober every night. And he tried, without ever actually apologizing, to make up for his outbursts by taking us
with him when he made the rounds of his sisters' and
brothers' houses, or by slipping us a dollar or two when

we left the house with friends.

My father protected himself with a kind of fake-gruff exterior which could be funny or intimidating, depending on the context, and which completely broke apart when his own father died, late on a June night in 1965. He summoned us to the table the next morning as we were about to leave for school. I was twelve, my brothers nine and seven, and, while we knew our grandfather was ill, we'd had no prior experience with death. My father had had no prior experience bringing news of death to his children, and when he sat in one of the kitchen chairs and gathered us around him, there were tears in his eyes and, on his face, a sad twitch we had never seen.

"God called Grandpa last night," he said, after a struggle.

We had no idea what this meant, why God should be calling Grandpa up on the phone, and why it should upset our father so much. Washed, combed, and lit with the anticipation of one of the year's final school days, the last thing we expected was that we would never again see the man who had lived beneath or beside us every day of our lives.

"God called Grandpa last night," my father repeated.

Now there was more trouble in his face, and my mother was wringing her hands as if to urge the words out of him, and his grief was so enormous and so pent-up, that even without any understanding of death we had a sense of something new and terrible invading our house.

"What do you mean, Pa?" I said, but by this point I was close to knowing.

"Grandpa died last night," he managed, finally. The fake-gruff exterior collapsed, the five of us huddled in its ruins, and wept.

Not long after that, the prestige and comfort of the Director's job began to lose some of its appeal for him. Perhaps it was the fresh sense of mortality he felt after his father's passing. Or perhaps there was some regret there, after all, at not having gone to Washington. My father had had a taste of the high life, a bit of fame and power, and perhaps, after a decade, the Industrial Accident Board had begun to look like just another sinecure.

Since his carrot-picking days, he'd cherished the dream of becoming a lawyer, and in the course of his duties at the Board, he'd rubbed shoulders with lawyers and judges day after day. And so, in 1966, at the age of fifty, he met with the Dean of Admissions of Suffolk Law School and convinced her to admit him without an undergraduate degree.

For the next four years he rose at six o'clock on weekdays, left the house at seven-thirty, made the forty-minute subway commute to downtown Boston, worked at the Board until five or five-thirty, attended classes at Suffolk from seven to ten, then rode the subway back to Revere. My mother met him at Beachmont station and drove him home, set the table again, cooked a second supper. At eleven o'clock, she went upstairs to bed, and he went down into the basement room he'd refinished, and hit the law books there until one or two A.M.

At Suffolk, an average grade of seventy was required to pass. My father's average in his first year was sixty-nine.

Suffolk gave him the choice of repeating the year or failing out of school. He repeated the year, moved his average up ten points, and made steady, unspectacular progress through the rest of his law school career. By the time of his graduation in 1970, he stood in the middle of his class, a B student, age fifty-four, with a family and a full-time day job as his extracurricular interests.

What a deep and resonant triumph it was for him, that graduation. What a party we threw. His mother, siblings, and in-laws came, all forty of our cousins, old family friends, new friends from law school, monsignors and mayors, bricklayers and hairdressers, neighbors who'd lived within shouting distance of us for thirty years on Essex Street without having any idea of my father's secret ambition. He rarely drank, but he drank that night. For the only time in my life I saw him slightly tipsy, dancing with my mother in the cellar room where he had spent so many studious hours.

When the celebration ended, he took a week off to putter around the house, then returned to work at the Board, studying at night and on weekends for the Bar Examination, which he took for the first time that fall. A score of one hundred out of a possible two hundred was required to pass; the examiners told him he had scored "in the high nineties."

Still working full-time, still maintaining the house and showing up at our baseball games, he took the bar a second time, and failed again. He failed a third time and a fourth, at six-month intervals, and by then even his closest friends were counseling surrender. You've made your point, they told him. You did something almost nobody else could have done at your age. Let it rest. But, for better or worse, he was not the type to let something rest. Not even close to the type. His customary response to those who advised him to give up the chase was a not very facetious: "Go to hell."

The twice-yearly notice from the Board of Massachusetts Bar Examiners had come to be a terrible ritual in our home: the buildup of fear and hope, the arrival of the letter, the bad news, which my father took stoically, clamping his teeth down on the stem of his pipe, staring out the kitchen window in a gray-headed, 220-pound silence, ashamed beyond any speaking of it.

The fifth such letter was delivered in March of 1973, on a dreary Saturday morning. My father had just taken the curtains from the living-room windows, my mother was in the kitchen washing the floor. Steve, Ken, and I were doing a fair imitation of dusting when we heard the mailman's tread on the front step. I retrieved the mail, saw the letter from the Bar Examiners, handed it over to my father, and retreated. He stood at the window in the cold spring light and turned the envelope over twice in his hands, preparing himself, stretching out those last minutes of hope. My mother waited in absolute silence in the kitchen. My brothers hovered near the top of the stairs; I stayed in the front hall, spying.

With an engineer's precision, he slid his letter-opener beneath the flap and drew out a single sheet. He unfolded it with one hand, scanned it, then looked up and out at Essex Street with an expression I could not read. Defiance? Anger? Reluctant surrender? For half a minute he stared out at the cars at the curb, the tilting telephone poles and rusting TV antennas, and then he pushed three words up through his throat in the general direction of my mother: "El, I passed." My mother shrieked, we ran to embrace him, we wept, we shook his hand, kissed him. For the rest of that day my brothers and I floated around the neighborhood in an ecstasy of pride and relief.

For several more years the sun of good fortune shone upon him. His many local friends sent him what law business they had, wills mostly, small troubles. One or two of the companies he'd worked with put him on retainer. He resigned from the Industrial Accident Board and accepted a part-time job as a Workers' Compensation Specialist at Revere City Hall, trying to sort out the truly injured from the professional fakers, wrangling with the city council on which he had once served, then, at home, earning more money in an evening than he'd previously earned in a week.

During the years of my father's law career, I was building up my own small business, a one-man painting and carpentry operation in northwestern Massachusetts and southern Vermont, three-and-a-half hours from Revere. Too poor, at first, to afford a vehicle, I kept my tools in a knapsack and rode to jobs on a ten-speed bicycle with my handsaw twanging and bouncing over the back wheel.

For six dollars an hour I replaced panes of glass, scraped and painted the soffits of old garages, patched ceilings, peeled up tile from rotted bathroom floors.

Nothing puzzled him more than this lifestyle of mine, this freedom and indigence. Here was a son who had earned both a bachelor's and master's degree from an Ivy League school, who had worked for the State Department behind the Iron Curtain, who, in his late twenties, held credentials admitting him to the choicest precincts of the non-Revere world. And what was he doing? Living in the woods rebuilding porches for old Vermonters, reading at night in the Williams College library because he and his wife could not afford to heat their apartment, nailing up clapboards in the freezing cold.

My claim that it was all temporary, that I was pursuing a writing career, made little impression on him. "When," he said to me during his one visit to the country, "are you going to take responsibility?" I thought of reminding him of his days climbing down into ditches, his pursuit—stubborn, illogical—of a life that suited him, in spite of the odds . . . but I made a joke instead, biding time it turned out I did not have.

The last time I saw him was in Revere in the summer of 1982. We'd bought a vehicle by then, an old repainted Sears van which he'd found for me at auction. Amanda and I had driven down to celebrate his sixty-sixth birthday, and I'd spent part of the weekend scraping and painting the front entrance of the house so that it would be more presentable to his clients. On the morning we were to head back home, I came down into the kitchen and found a hundred-dollar bill on the table and a note. Tender phrases were never a specialty of my father's. He was not a rough man by any means, but neither was he comfortable with the more delicate aspects of human relationship, not, in any case, where his sons were concerned. (When I was going out on dates in my college years, he would watch me combing my hair and spraying deodorant, would hand me the keys to his Pontiac, slip me ten bucks, and say: "Be careful"—the closest we ever came to a father-son talk on sexuality.)

Tender expressions were not his specialty, but that note was filled with tenderness. How glad he and my mother were that we visited, how grateful for the work I'd done, how much they loved Amanda, and so on. All of this folded around a hundred dollars, the equivalent, in those lean years, of my weekly income. Amanda came downstairs and I said to her, "Look at this, will you? My father, huh?"

I didn't realize that he had not yet left for his job at City Hall, and was standing a few feet away at the back door, staring out into the yard. He made a small coughing sound, and I saw him, and we went through the usual ritual of me refusing the money and him refusing to take it back three or four times before I finally folded the note and cash into my wallet, thanked him, and kissed him good-bye.

For two months the note remained there. One day in July I decided I was being sentimental or superstitious— unmanly traits—and threw it into a trash barrel on a beach on Long Island.

Two weeks later I was painting a house in Williamstown, up on a ladder in the bright morning, when I heard a car pull to the curb and saw my wife get out. Amanda crossed the lawn and stopped at the foot of the ladder.

"Be down in a minute," I said. "Just let me finish this piece of trim before the sun comes around."

"Come down now," she said.

"One second, I just—"

"Come down now, Rol."

I climbed down and stood facing her. "Bad news," she said.

He died in his sleep, with no sign of the struggle that had marked so much of his life, and for months and months after his death I dreamt of him regularly—straightforward, extremely vivid dreams that did not require the assistance of an analyst to interpret. In one, he was sitting in the back seat of a white limousine, at the passenger side window, and I saw the limo pull out of a drive way and sprinted after it, waving and waving, calling out, "Good-bye, Pa. Good-bye. Good-bye!" But he was looking straight ahead, smiling, and didn't see me.

Now, a few years shy of the age when my father decided to attend law school, I occasionally dream of him still. Sometimes we argue, sometimes I tease him about not visiting us. He often smiles in these dreams, but rarely speaks. Each year that passes, each incremental diminution of my own powers, brings a sharper understanding of the force of his will, the effort and self-belief and self-sacrifice and pure stubbornness that can be read between the lines of his resume. I have, it turns out, inherited a portion of his discipline, but what matters more to me is his gift of a sense of perspective, what he would have called his "faith," a certain spiritual or psychological ballast that holds a person close to some center line, even amidst the greatest victories and the deepest bitterness. I keep a framed photo of him on the wall in the room where I write, and say a word to it from time to time, when things are going very badly, or very well.

A Little Down Time

By the time I reached the age of sixteen I had
been hospitalized three times, twice for mysterious digestive problems, and once for an injury to my right eye. The
stomach troubles began shortly after I turned three, and
went on, unsolved, for ten years. Every month or so during that period I would be stricken with a severe pain in,
the lower part of my abdomen, a pain that was immune to
the soothing effects of aspirin, warm washcloths, and the
tender ministrations of my mother, father, and grandparents. Hands between my knees, or clutched in fists at my
sides, I would curl up on the divan (as we called it then) or
in the back seat of my parents' Pontiac, and whimper—
when I was younger—or, when I grew too old for that,
grit my teeth and let out an occasional moan. It was a terrible pain, deep and sharp. It radiated into my pelvis and
penis, and made me not want to eat or move for the hour
and a half or two hours between the time it suddenly arrived and the time it suddenly disappeared.

It should have been obvious to everyone involved that there was a psychological component to these attacks. When I was five years old I had one on Halloween night, and wasn't able to go out trick-or-treating. I remember sitting on the top step of our second-floor apartment, dressed in my ghost costume, doubled over with pain, torn between the sweet tug of the streets and the indolent release of the sickbed. Some years later, I remember curling into a miserable ball in the corner of the car's back seat while my brothers and father rode the amusements at a local fair. And watching my favorite football team, the New York Giants, lose a close game, the tense last few minutes of which brought on another awful two-hour battle.

It ought to have been clear enough to the various doctors who treated me that I was a nervous sort of boy, and that the excitement of Halloween or an amusement park was enough to trigger the odd response in my intestines. But all this began in the fifties, when "stress" was not yet a household word, never mind a medical diagnosis. And there were plenty of holidays, amusement park visits, and close football games when I felt nothing more than the ordinary tickle of nervousness beneath my belt buckle. It was a capricious, mysterious illness, the source of which did not reveal itself to doctors' probing fingers, did not leave any traces on the dozens of X rays that were taken; a malady that arrived and departed on a schedule of its own making, leaving me wrung out, exhausted, hungry, and bathed in a mixture of fear and pride. Fear, because the memory of the pain was fresh and I knew it would return—in two weeks, in a month. And pride, a perverse and stubborn pride, because I knew I had endured something difficult, something that went beyond the ordinary requirements of childhood.

It seems to me now that the suffering of children has more in common with the suffering of the very old and the dying than with the aches and illnesses of middle adulthood. Ordinarily healthy middle-aged adults worry over their physical traumas, adding a thick layer of mental torment: how much it will cost; how many days of work, or running, or tennis, will be missed; what the cause might be—some sort of undiscovered cancer? Children and the dying and the very ill are better at relinquishing control over the situation—children because they are well practiced in the difficult art of yielding to another's will, and the very ill and the dying because they have fought and fought, for months, for years, and at last the muscle of their hope has given way under the long assault of agony or incapacity. Though their suffering is as real and as painful, they suffer dumbly, quietly, like animals. They seem to understand instinctively—or finally—that pain and suffering have no explanation. There may be a scientific reason—a tumor, a bacteria, a blocked vessel—but the source of that tumor or blockage remains utterly veiled.

Why me? Most of us ask when we are incapacitated or inconvenienced, whereas the dying person eventually stops asking, and the child has not yet learned to.

In their search for an answer and a cure, my parents brought me to the family pediatrician, and then to specialists in Boston. Questions, X rays, syrups and tablets, fluoroscopes, new diets—nothing worked: the pain arrived, I writhed and moaned and sweated, the pain left.

When I was seven, I was admitted to the Brooks Hospital near Boston, a small, private, old-fashioned place with a brick exterior and squeaking linoleum floors. By then I was seeing a new specialist, said to be the doctor of one of Boston's most famous men, Ted Williams. I remember this doctor complaining to my mother that most of the problems with kids came from the fact that they ate too much pizza and Coke, and I remember that he settled on a diagnosis of "pancreatitis," and put me on a strict diet that I mostly adhered to, and that helped me not at all. When he learned that his treatment had failed, he sent me to the hospital for more tests. There, at Brooks, I made friends with a man who'd lost half of one arm when a crane cable snapped, recoiled, and sliced through his elbow. The original surgery didn't stop the spread of gangrene up his arm, and he told me he kept having to return to the hospital to have another inch or so cut from his stump. While there was something horrifying in this image—it haunted me for weeks afterwards: the sense of rotting flesh, of a failed operation, of having to come back to the hospital again and have another small piece of yourself cut away and discarded; the sense of a cable as thick as my arm snapping under the pressure of its load and whipsawing through the air, breaking the window of the cabin in which my friend had sat, slicing through bone like a jackknife through a milkweed stalk—the man and I became good friends and I liked visiting him and listening to his stories.

Early on my second morning at Brooks a nurse came into my room and announced in her pleasant nurse's voice: "We're going to give you an enema now."

"What's an enema?" I said.

"An enema is where we put a tube into your bummy and pour water in and it makes you have to go to the bathroom right away."

"You're not going to do that," I told her.

"Yes, we are. The doctor says we have to."

"No you aren't."

"We are, though."

She prevailed. Afterwards I walked down to my friend's room, carrying the humiliation of that procedure with me, and it linked us in a certain way, as if both of us were at the mercy of a greater force that was only inter-mittently kind. He spoke to me as if I were grown up, and that little dose of mutual respect and affection took the edge off of things.

Two years later I was hospitalized again, on the orders of a different doctor, with a different diagnosis for the same trouble. This physician was quite sure the problem stemmed from an inflamed appendix, so I checked into the Children's Hospital to have the offending part re-moved. Of those three days I remember only that a younger boy in one of the beds in my room told the nurse that bacon was his favorite fruit, and that, late one night, I bit through the glass thermometer and caused a ruckus.

It was after midnight. For some reason, the nurse had been instructed to wake me up at that hour and take my temperature. She settled the thermometer under my tongue, told me to be sure not to touch it with my hands, and left on her rounds. The instrument grew slippery with saliva. Careful not to reach up and adjust it, I was maneuvering it back and forth with my lips, trying to get a more solid grip, when I felt it slipping out of my mouth. So I bit down. And it broke. And the nurse returned to find me sitting stoically still, with a mouth full of glass and mercury. A small panic ensued: announcements over the loudspeaker, doctors hurrying into the room and yelling at me not to swallow, to keep my mouth open, to stay still while they picked the pieces of glass out, washed my tongue, gums, and teeth, fed me some concoction to protect my innards from the effects of mercury.

On the night before the operation I caught a cold, and the procedure was postponed, and then canceled, and I am in possession of my appendix to this day.

By the time I was fifteen the mysterious digestive problem had cured itself. I had become, more or less, an ordinary teenager: I reluctantly wore eyeglasses in the classroom, cared more about friends than grades, played sports, listened to rock and roll, and believed with unquestioned certainty that the reins with which my parents guided me were being held too tightly.

The real torment of those years, for me, was that I had not yet reached puberty. From the seventh through the tenth grade I was either the shortest or second-to-shortest boy in all my classes, shorter than most of the girls as well. My muscles were a child's muscles, and with them I was supposed to compete—on the baseball diamond, in the swimming pool, in playground fistfights—with boys who shaved and did twenty pull-ups and talked about their adventures with girls in terms that baffled me.

I attended Catholic school for the ninth and tenth grades, and I recall one of the Xavierian Brothers there telling us that, by age fourteen, 98 percent of boys have masturbated. This bit of information was given to us during religion class, and was meant to assure us that we were not all condemned to hell. It was intended as an act of kindness, and, in my case, it would have been received that way, except for the fact that, not only had I not masturbated yet, I had not the slightest idea what the term actually meant. I had heard it, of course, and all its many slang equivalents. And I had joked with my friends about it, adopting the proper tone and lingo as part of the armor of those years. But my body was a child's body, small and hairless, a stranger to lust. I was a prisoner in the oddball 2 percent.

At last, during the summer of 1968, that murderous and shameful summer in the life of America, my body began to mature. In June a few hairs sprouted over my top lip and under my arms, I grew an inch or two and was now, finally, at five feet five inches, as tall as my mother. One very hot Friday in the middle of July, my friend Michael Capone and I (he was on the short side, too, and loved sports, and hated fighting, so we were natural allies) walked down to the tennis courts for nine innings of stickball. Stickball is a game perfectly suited to summer in the city. It costs next to nothing—no cleats or uniform, no glove or cap; a broomstick for a bat and a twenty-five-cent rubber ball. You have to throw and hit, but you don't have to run. You need only a thin corridor of space and a concrete wall on which to paint your strike zone. We could play for hours, Michael and I, embellishing the basic action with an elaborate play-by-play, comparing ourselves to Red Sox and Yankee stars. "Maris lines one deep, deep . . . off the top of the fence in right center!"

"It's three and two. Monboquette winds and throws . . and catches the corner with a wicked curve."

We played one man to a team. There were half-a-dozen strike zones marked on the green cinderblock wall, and a fifteen-foot-high chain-link fence about fifty yards away. A ball hit against the top half of the fence counted as a triple, the bottom half a double, anything else in fair territory was a single—unless the pitcher fielded a ground ball or caught a pop-up. Under this system, with just one fielder, so much open space, and such a short distance to home-run territory, an inning could go on for the better part of half an hour, and a game could last all morning or afternoon.

Michael and I were evenly matched and temperamentally well suited. We had arrived at the courts early enough to claim the best strike zone, and were in the middle of our sweaty game when I wound up to throw a pitch and felt something hit the side of my face with tremendous force. The impact knocked me flat on my back, the pain was immediate and overwhelming, and I thought, at first, that some old enemy from junior high had walked up and blindsided me with a right hook. I lay there on the tar, close to passing out, unable to move. "Oh, man," Michael said, when he ran up. "Johnny DiGenova hit a line drive.

You didn't see it, did you? Man, look at your eye!"

Johnny DiGenova came over to apologize. "Oh boy," he said under his breath when he saw me. After several minutes I sat up, then stood, the pain resonating in my skull and the bones of the right side of my face. Michael escorted me to a drinking fountain at the softball diamond, and I splashed cold water into the eye for a long time. But when I straightened up and wiped a sleeve across my face I still could not see half the world.

It was five blocks to my house. Michael stayed close to me the whole way, helped me up the stairs, and, before heading home, asked for the twentieth time if I was sure I didn't want him to call the ambulance or something. I slipped into the empty house and lay down on the divan with an ice cube wrapped in a washcloth pressed against my eye. In a little while my middle brother Steven came home and asked me to show him what had happened. I lifted the washcloth away and made him swear he wouldn't call our mother—who was taking care of her own mother a few miles away—or tell anyone what had happened. What my motivation for secrecy was, I am, not sure. All kinds of shame haunt the adolescent boy or girl. The most neutral events contain within them the potential for humiliation, as if the fourteen-year-old is so determined to make himself an adult by the force of his will that he refuses to acknowledge anything even remotely resembling weakness or childishness. In great pain though I was, the last thing I wanted at that moment was the fuss and sympathy of my mother.

But, after swearing not to tell anyone, Steve sneaked

35

upstairs, dialed the number of my grandmother's house and, as I found out later, said, "Ma, Rolly's eye is all blood inside. He's laying on the couch with ice on it. You should see it, Ma."

It took my mother about eight minutes to get home, and about another three minutes to force me into the Pontiac and drive me to Dr. Berson's office in Chelsea. It took Dr. Berson about four minutes to examine the eye and tell my mother to drive me into Boston to the Massachusetts Eye and Ear emergency room. He would call ahead, he said. They'd be expecting me.

But on the way into town (as we called Boston then) we became entangled in a world-class Friday-afternoon traffic jam on the Mystic River Bridge. By that time the pain had filled my skull and neck like molten metal, and that hour stands in my memory, still, as one of the longest of my life.

There was a crowd in the emergency room, and several cases more serious than mine. We waited and waited. I began to go into shock. Fortunately, my mother had had enough experience in hospitals, and around doctors, to recognize the symptoms, and had enough brashness about her to insist that the nurse wrap me in blankets and find a doctor who would see me right away.

In a little while I had been given some medicine for the pain and was set up in a bed on one of the hospital's upper floors. The eye specialist, we were told, had been on his way to Cape Cod for a summer weekend, but had turned around and would be back to examine me within the hour. Until then, I should stay flat on my back with both eyes covered, and try not to move.

Telling a fourteen-year-old not to move is like telling the earth not to rotate. I was in pain, impatient with the confinement of the last few hours, and when the man in the next bed began telling me the story of his injury (he was prying a metal outlet plate from his mother's wall with a screwdriver when the plate snapped and a piece of it flew into his eye) I rolled halfway over toward his voice.

Dr. Leibman strode into the room and found me that way—knees up, torso partially twisted. Probably he was in a sour mood to begin with, having been caught in the middle of his Friday afternoon getaway, his mind filled with thoughts of a sunny beach and a lobster dinner. With both my parents sitting in a worried posture by the bed, he shouted and lectured. Didn't I know I had an internal hemorrhage of the retina? Hadn't the nurses and the other doctors told me to remain absolutely still, not even to pull my knees up? Didn't I realize I was on the verge of losing the sight in my right eye?

No was the answer to the first and third questions. But at least now we understood the situation. Johnny DiGenova's line drive had hit the side of my eyeball with such force that it had caused a hemorrhage around the retinal nerve. The hemorrhage would heal itself, if I stayed absolutely still and kept my eyes covered for three days and nights. But if I moved, if there were a second hemorrhage, then I would likely be blind in that eye for life.

What an ordeal it was to follow Dr. Leibman's instructions. What an eternity of a weekend. The darkness, the boredom, the way the muscles of my back and legs twitched and cried out. Every few hours a nurse would come into the room and hand me a pitcher to pee into, spoon some food into my mouth, give me some medicine for the pain. My parents visited, my brothers, a cousin and his wife. ("Rolly, what do you do if you have to go to the bathroom?" the cousin asked me, a question that still seems to me the epitome of insensitivity. And I lied, saying casually that they allowed me to stand up just for that—because I was too embarrassed to talk about pitchers and bedpans.)

When word spread through the family that I might lose the vision in my right eye, my parents, grandparents, cousins, aunts and uncles began flooding the Catholic airwaves with prayers. We believed that there had been a martyr named Lucy who'd let her eyes be cut out rather than renounce her faith, and, during that weekend, we pleaded with her to help my hemorrhage heal.

Roman Catholicism has a sacred hierarchy that roughly resembles the President of the United States and his cabinet. Since life is so complex, the Lord divides up his responsibilities, appointing Saint Lucy to preside over eye troubles, Saint Jude to preside over impossible cases, Saint Blaise to watch over illnesses of the throat, Saint Anthony to help find lost articles, and so on. Of all the various quirks of Catholicism, this seems the easiest to mock. That there should be some Anthony up in the sky with nothing better to do than send down subtle hints as to the location of misplaced gloves and favorite fountain pens. That Lucy should be up there with him, listening to the wishes of the Merullo family, and then going in to her regular Saturday morning appointment with God and pleading the case of a Revere kid who got hurt playing stickball. Even the idea that there should be a caring God presiding over this cauldron of agony and dismemberment, of torture and premature death, and that our whispered petitions might sway Him one way or another—it cuts against the grain of logic.

But logic and faith have their roots in different parts of the brain: the family prayed and prayed. I stayed on my back from Friday afternoon through Monday morning; the hemorrhage healed itself Doctor Leibman, kinder now after his weekend of rest and my weekend of obedience, took off the bandages, shone lights in my eyes, and declared me fit to return home.

But the story does not quite end there. For one thing, when my mother came to take me home she said I seemed to have sprouted over the weekend. Other relatives we visited that day said the same thing. At home, my brothers and I had drawn pencil lines on a part of the back hallway wall to track our growth, and when I stood there, and let my mother make another mark, and stepped away, it turned out I'd grown three inches. Some combination of all that bedrest and the urgency in my bones had propelled me out of the hell of undersized boyhood. Three inches in a weekend. Seven inches, in all, over the course of that summer. I grew and grew, adding height even as late as my freshman year in college, and ending up a quarter inch shy of six feet.

Perhaps because he'd never seen me standing up, Dr. Leibman did not remark the change in height when I arrived at his office for the one-month checkup. He was a white-haired, jowly fellow, ready for retirement, no doubt, and his office manner was even kinder than what I'd seen on my last day in the hospital. He asked the usual questions and went through the usual tests with his charts and lights. When that was finished, he sat me down again opposite his desk and said, "Young man, I've been practicing medicine for forty years and I've never seen a case like yours. Not only has the injured eye completely healed, but your vision, which, according to these records, had been steadily deteriorating over the past five years, has improved to the point where it is better than what we consider perfect. Now that wouldn't be so amazing if it had happened only in the damaged eye—sometimes a trauma like the one you sustained will correct the shape of the lens and improve vision. But your other eye is now better than perfect as well. I'm puzzled, I'm baffled. You can go home and throw your eyeglasses away." I did that, with some ceremony, and thirty-two years later have yet to buy another pair.

This was, of course, all the evidence my family needed. Another million or so prayers—of thanks, this time—were sent up toward Saint Lucy. Some of them, even now, come from me, a practicing Buddhist. Who can say there isn't a saintly woman in the ether looking down on us? Who knows why she and her colleagues accede to some requests and ignore others? Who can possibly understand why crane cables snap in just such a way to cut off a man's arm, why children fall ill and die, why tyrants rise from the ashes of bad history and torture and murder their way through a German, Cambodian, or Iraqi generation, why all of us suffer as we do?

The reason behind our pain lies at the very heart of the puzzle that is human existence, hidden there behind dark glass, veiled, impenetrable, a thorn in the boot of the most confident theorists. Our only response, it seems to me, on those occasions when the instruments of logic and science have been tried and found wanting, is a kind of eight-year-old's honest anger at the unfairness of it all, and an innocent hope that it leads us, eventually, to some clearer view of the way things really are.

My Two Heavens

"So, I saw from your biographical material that you grew up in Revere and then went to Exeter Academy. What was that like?"

This question was put to me ten years ago by a newspaper reporter in a small restaurant not far from where I live. My first book had just been published, and he had been sent to do an interview, and he seemed like a decent man with no hidden agenda driving him.

But something in the question sounded an old suspicious note in me. It seemed weighted with all sorts of assumptions and judgments—that Revere was a certain kind of place, that Phillips Exeter was a certain kind of place, that growing up in one and going to school in the other was the equivalent of changing blood type at age fifteen.

What was that like?

I once heard someone draw a comparison between Revere, Massachusetts, and Brooklyn, New York: close to the heart of a metropolis and yet in possession of a distinctly separate identity; houses pushed tight together on busy streets with cars parked wherever their owners can find a place for them; small, almost-private yards with vegetable gardens, concrete saints, and an air of charged domesticity. Revere is much smaller, but the two places have matching reputations for toughness and good food, a paucity of the tranquility one finds in the leafy suburbs, a vibrancy the leafy suburbs often lack.

Exeter Academy, on the other hand (or Phillips Exeter Academy, as it is formally known) has never once in its 218-year history been linked in such a way with Brooklyn. Set on 471 acres in southeastern New Hampshire, composed of 115 stately red-brick buildings separated by groomed lawns, home to 1,000 very bright and, in some cases, extremely wealthy teenagers from 44 states and 27 foreign countries, Exeter looks more like a heaven for honor roll students than a high school. The atmosphere cannot in any sense of the word be described as rough, the food is not good (at least when I was a student there; this may have changed), one is not very likely to come across people arguing over a parking space.

So it would seem that the reporter was perfectly within his rights to have led off with such a question, and given it such pointed intonation. The problem for me was that I believed I could sense the images that leapt to mind when he thought "Revere" and "Exeter," and I did not like them. He had not spent much time in either place, I was pretty sure, and yet he spoke as if he knew them. All of us do this. When we hear "South Central L.A." or "Beverly Hills," "Westchester" or "Mississippi" a whole menagerie of images comes to mind. This may be inevitable, and it is often harmless. But our assumptions about other places are usually too simple to hold much truth, and the foundation on which label, stereotype, and reputation are constructed is almost always a flimsy thing, cobbled together from bits of fact, hearsay, and prejudice.

What was *that* like?

For a kid growing up in the 1950s and 1960s, Revere was a kind of working-class heaven, that's what it was like. A lot of people have sweet feelings about the territory of their childhood. That, I would guess, has more to do with the perceiving instrument than with the object perceived. But those of us who grew up in Revere like to believe there was a special light shining on our particular paradise. And perhaps there was. After all, how many kids have a beach and an amusement park in their front yard?

Revere Beach in those years was a straightforward, gritty place, multicultural long before the word came into vogue. I do, in fact, remember arguments over parking spaces there along the boardwalk. I also remember standing with my uncle neck-deep in water clear as glass, feeling about with our feet for sea snails the size of apricots, which we put into a bucket and carried home for supper. I remember three-mile walks along fine gray sand, and gangs of friends playing blockball, and, on the west side of the Boulevard, a long stretch of food stands, amusement rides, and games of chance.

In those days, the early 1960s, the roller coaster was rickety, and the tattooed attendants at the bumper-car ride might have benefited from some of the good anti-aggression drugs available now. But you did not have to buy a ticket to get into this amusement park. You did not have to pay three times as much for a hot dog as you would in an ordinary restaurant. If you wanted to give your kids a few hours of fun, you did not need round-trip airfare to Orlando.

In the summertime we had the Wild Mouse and the Virginia Reel, snake-hunting at May Rock, and fistfights on the stickball courts that got as much billing, locally, as Liston-Clay in Lewiston. In winter there were street hockey games in front of the house, where the puck was a pink rubber ball and the goal two soup cans set six feet apart. If you were the goalie and having a rough day, you might nudge the cans an inch or two closer to each other, give yourself that slight mathematical edge. Of course, in my club of friends there were arguments and shifting allegiances, and, on our street, a few neighbors who seemed to think we had no right to use the alleyways behind their garages as hiding places. But, winter and summer, no one went in for supper until they'd been called three or four times.

Even such a place, though, cannot remain a paradise after a certain age. It seemed to me that as my friends and I were pooled together into larger schools, the demands on our teachers' patience and energy stretched them past their limits. Once, at the start of eighth-grade music class, a student one row over from me was pushed out the window. The teacher did not seem to notice, or—perhaps because we were only half a story off the pavement, and the student had been giving him some trouble—did not seem to care. The girls, and then the boys, grew like trees in the rainforest, leaving me and one or two other late-bloomers stranded in a smooth-skinned dwarfdom. On a particularly depressing March afternoon, one of the tallest girls somehow got hold of my left penny-loafer and held it above her head while I reached and jumped in a fit of futility. In such a place there was no advantage to being a short boy with skinny arms, believe me. Neither was there any great advantage, in McKinley Junior High School at least, to being seen carrying home textbooks, or raising a hand to answer a teacher's question.

Some of my friends navigated those rough waters with more dignity than I did—by learning not to care so much what someone else said about the books or the raised hand; or by mastering the courses in juvenile delinquency, given at no charge, by high school kids on the corner. But I felt myself sinking by the week, torn, like so many other adolescents (and so many adults), between the urge for popularity and the intimate counsel of the soul. After some kind of standardized IQ test, the assistant principal called me into his office and said all kinds of nice things… every word of which I would have traded for a glance from the girl who sat next to me in algebra, or three or four more inches in height.

So, in the space of a year, my paradise had evaporated. But during that time something happened that, though I did not see it, and would not hear about it for thirty years, changed the flight-line of my fate. As my mother tells the story, a woman came up to her at some social event and said "Your son shouldn't be in school here, you should get him out." This was not a friend of the family, but the wife of a casual acquaintance. I had never met the woman, and have not met her still. To this day I cannot explain what moved her to take such liberties, or to care so much about someone she did not know, except by noting that, in Revere, neither straightforwardness nor kindness is ever in short supply. Whatever the reason, she said it, and my mother listened, and talked to my father, and from that day forward they began a process of sending away for catalogs and application forms, driving me to SAT tests, and then getting a job, in my mother's case, and taking out loans in my father's. They turned themselves into a sort of parental rocket engine, burning up their own lives so that I might be propelled into some other orbit we could barely imagine but which was supposed to be better.

After two years as a commuting student at St. John's Prep in Danvers, a Catholic high school, my new orbit turned out to be The Phillips Exeter Academy, where the buildings, given by rich donors, carried names you were not likely to come across in the Revere phone book, where some boys had grandfathers and even great-grandfathers on the alumni rolls, and where we wore a sport coat and tie to classes six days a week.

What was that like? The reporter would have guessed it to be a shocking adjustment for a working-class fifteen-year-old who, except for one trip to the World's Fair, had never been more than seventy-five miles from Revere, a kid who had grown up eating his salad and meat with the same fork. But, as is usually the case, the truth, the prickly individual truth, is twenty times more complicated than that.

To begin with, I was so, naive at age fifteen that I had no idea what being wealthy really meant, no sense whatsoever of the vast distance between the lives of the DuPonts or the Achesons—Exeter classmates—and my life. Friends in the dorm taught me bridge, I taught them the Italian card game *briscola*. They went skiing in Switzerland on winter vacation, my family made day trips into Boston to go to the Museum of Science, and had pizza afterwards at Bill Ash's on the beach. Their parents had cocktail hour; my parents had an hour that was called Home from Work and Need To Make Supper. Those are the familiar symbols that stand for the differences between the laboring class and the inheritance class. Those are the sitcom clichés, but they meant nothing to me at that age. Even the fact that as a scholarship boy (beneficiary of a fund established by Walter Brown, the late Boston Celtics owner), I was required to wait on faculty tables at dinner, carried no special weight. That practice has since been discontinued at Exeter, but honestly, I did not resent it then or feel singled out.

Indeed, the Academy is so financially healthy (an endowment of $387 million, more than most colleges) that it has always had a good record of admitting middle-class and poor kids. I did not care about that either.

What I cared about was that my roommate was a good guy, that I could play hockey every winter day on a real ice rink, make the JV baseball team, walk alone in the woods. It meant something to me that the classes were never larger than thirteen, and that we sat around an oval table with the teacher instead of facing him in rows. It made me feel good that just about everyone took home books and studied hard for tests. There was rifle club, chess club, student council, visits from my parents and brothers every Sunday with boxes of cookies from a bakery back home. There were mixers with Pingree, games against Andover, people from all over the world to talk to. I had fled one paradise and stumbled into another.

What difficulties I encountered had to do with the strict rules and unappetizing food. What sense of class dislocation I felt came from the teachers, dedicated as they were, who seemed to me to be members of another species with their tweed sport coats and Anglo-Saxon names. Compared to the adults I was used to at home, these men moved with a different kind of confidence, talked more formally, seemed to have very different sets of assumptions about life. I felt this keenly, but, in those days, did not have the vocabulary for explaining it to myself.

Those days, as they say, are gone. Almost thirty years have passed, and the naiveté about class distinctions disappeared long ago—otherwise the reporter's perfectly ordinary question would never have struck me as it did. The spacecraft in which my parents launched me is scratched and dented and plastered with partly erased copies of every imaginable label and judgment. I have eaten from the tree of the knowledge of rich and not so rich. I can no longer claim full citizenship in either paradise.

Recently I went back to Exeter to see, among other things, how the perceiver and the object of perception might have changed.

The answer, in the latter instance at least, is—not much. Though the Exeter Inn is now "The Inn at Exeter," and the nearby Catholic Church bills itself as "A Catholic Community," and though the sub shop where I used to console myself after dinner four nights a week has been turned into a bicycle store, the school itself has changed remarkably little over three decades. There is a Dean of Multicultural Affairs now; and a sign in the school bookstore announcing that "a closed-circuit camera is in operation"; and plastic-wrapped muffins at the snack bar in place of the homemade cinnamon buns we used to think about with such wonderful anticipation during chapel. Most striking, to my eye, was the presence of girls on campus (49 percent of the student body), and of so many nonwhite students. Important changes, but, in another way, still in the realm of labels, surfaces. In a deeper sense, the school is what it was: a solid, staid institution nestled in the bosom of privilege.

On that afternoon, I walked back and forth across the campus in a comfortable anonymity, catching sight, now and then, of the half-recognized faces of elderly teachers and deans. The Academy bell sounded—I had forgotten how elegantly it marked the hours. The wind nipped at my cheeks and neck—I had forgotten how cold it could be there, just south of the mountains and west of the sea. There were fresh copies of the *Wall Street Journal* in the school post office, and posters about a march for the homeless, and the grounds and buildings were beautifully maintained—things I never would have noticed, labeled, or cared about, in my younger days.

Because I had been an embarrassingly bad Russian student at Exeter, and later, in a kind of revenge, had gone to work in the Soviet Union for several years and learned to speak the language fluently, I asked to sit in on a Russian class. The class was taught by a sweet and gifted woman named Inna, who had emigrated from Kiev only a few years before. While her students wrote out complicated narratives in teams of two, Inna and I spent a few minutes talking, in Russian, about what it has been like for her to leave the former USSR, her family, her way of life, and move here to this American heaven. *"Proshlova nyet,"* she said her friends tell her when she talks about longing to go back for a visit: "The past is no more." But we talked about it anyway.

Afterwards, I walked over to the massive sports complex and found the faces of friends in the varsity team pictures that line the walls. Gods they had been to me in 1970, and here they were, looking like kids. Studying their faces, I recalled a night just before spring vacation, senior year, when a janitor let two friends and me into the locked complex and onto one of the rinks, long after the building was supposed to be off-limits to us. Three intramural stars with a whole sheet of new ice to ourselves—so far from the asphalt rink of my childhood—we skated and passed and invented spectacular plays until we could barely stand.

I walked out of the memory of that moment and onto the playing fields in a late-afternoon winter sun, stood for a few seconds at shortstop on the baseball diamond, went on as far as the river in a vapor of other memories, mostly good. But some buried emotion was stirring as I made my way back across the patches of ice and mud. Some sleeping beast had been knocked awake.

In the last hour of daylight, I paid a visit to the library, an architectural gem of a building with very clean windows and students at work in the carrels. The librarian left her desk to take me upstairs to the alumni collection, meticulously maintained in glass-fronted cases, shelf after shelf of Vidal, Irving, Agee, and the lesser knowns. "We'd be pleased if you'd sign your books," she said generously, and I did so. Downstairs again, we chatted for a little while on the oriental carpet, but I was distracted, deferential, self-conscious, broadsided by a volley of unexpected feelings so powerful I had difficulty putting two sentences together. This was more than mere nostalgia, deeper than that. Unless by nostalgia one means the sudden understanding that life is a series of exultations, each one fated to bloom for an hour or a month or a decade, and then wither.

I lingered in the lobby, trying to let the feeling settle, but it did not settle. I went outside to my car as the sun was going down, boys and girls holding hands on their way to dinner, students who looked as if their grandparents had gone here, students who didn't. I stood there for two minutes with the Academy bell tolling, and it occurred to me that all the time I'd spent working in the Soviet Union might have been my way of reaching back for a bit of what privilege always seems to wash out of a life. Soul, it might be called, or just honest suffering. It occurred to me that the Russian teacher and I had led very different lives with parallel trajectories—from a soulful, earthy simplicity toward something softer and richer, something said to resemble success. From louder laughter to quieter, neighbors in your parking space to neighbors beyond the trees, the Exeter Inn to the Inn at Exeter. So many people have made a similar voyage.

Given the chance, I would not go back now to my home place to live—*proshlova nyet*—and neither would she; we are lucky and happy in our lives. But there is a price to be paid for having left those places, and no matter what else happens we will always carry that invisible weight, that small sorrow. A ruble in the billfold, a beach stone in the briefcase of success.

That's what it's like.

Summer School

In 19̶1̶1̶ *1971*, the summer after my senior year in high school, I worked as part of the crew that was putting up Boston's John Hancock Tower, a skyscraper that had more than its share of problems in the early going. I. M. Pei's striking, blue-glass building—at sixty-two stories it is the city's tallest, even today—was about midway through its extremely troubled birth when I signed on in June. It was not exactly a construction job, not even work in the strictest sense. Truer to say, my father (whose generosity I had not yet started to resist) knew somebody who knew somebody, who arranged for me to get a paycheck for sitting in the engineer's trailer in Copley Square five days a week, doing the occasional odd job.

At first I felt uncomfortable there, and somewhat guilty. Dressed in steel-toed boots and Dickey work shirt and pants, I was a kind of impostor on the construction site, a naive prep school graduate with clear skin and soft hands surrounded by hard-drinking, hard-living iron-workers—a kid among men. There was a plain metal desk

54

in the trailer, at which I sat from eight to four-thirty, doodling, fidgeting, killing time. The project superintendent, Alex, had an office at one end of our hot little tin box, and the bookkeeper, Rico, had his office– doorless —at the other. Between them in the trailer's torso were two desks, a window looking out on Saint James Street, a quiet clutter of blueprints, hard hats, and suede gloves. This territory belonged to the two main engineers on the job—Nelson and Bird—and to me.

My days were a blend of dread and boredom. For hours at a time there would be nothing at all to do, or nothing but make-work—walking down to Flash's Deli at noon to buy sandwiches for Alex and Bird, sorting paychecks into envelopes, tallying up columns of figures for Rico or one of the engineers. And then, in the afternoon usually, Bird or Nelson would bang into the trailer and ask if I didn't want to accompany them "Upstairs."

We'd crowd into the rickety construction elevator, its walls only plywood and chain-link, and stare out over the city as a system of cables carried us up and up. Work had gone beyond the fiftieth story by then. The concrete floors had been poured, but above the fifteenth floor there were no walls, nothing in the stairwells and elevator shafts but air and, for the inattentive, trouble. In my boots and hard hat I followed the engineers from place to place, standing idly by as they pored over plans, took measurements, or argued a point with the foreman while stiff winds whipped across the workspace, and rivet-guns rattled, and ant-sized yellow taxis crept along beside the doors of Trinity Church, eight hundred feet below. From the moment I heard the word "Upstairs" to the moment the elevator brought us back down to ground level, my chest would be fluttering, my eyes flickering, my world a suddenly unpredictable and slightly swaying place. I did my best not to show any of this, of course. The men around me were walking on beams—something I was never asked to try—sweating, cursing, actually working for their money. The least I could do was keep the fear out of my face.

Despite their shared occupation, Bird and Nelson were totally different types: the former straitlaced, smart, and young; Nelson toothless, drunk some of the time, lurching toward retirement, and fond, as were many of the crew, of killing off six-packs in the evenings, or whoring in the Combat Zone. Bird provided an orientation to the jobsite, my first lessons. But, as the summer wore on, it was Nelson who spent more time with me. Perhaps something in my predicament—hours passed in repetitive work, an uncertain future looming—reminded him of himself, or perhaps there simply were no better conversational options. Whatever the reason, he did what he could to ease my tedium, providing crude if sketchy accounts of his Combat Zone debacles, asking now and then about my love life or my schooling. "There's a copy of the Markee there in your desk drawer," he said once, when he came into the trailer and found me caught again in my tin-walled boredom. "Check it out, why don't you. Pass the time."

The Markee, it turned out, was the Marquis de Sade, a well-thumbed copy of which Nelson kept in the desk and referred to from time to time when faced with a particularly thorny cantilever calculation. There were some pornographic cartoons in the drawer, as well—twenty or thirty Xeroxed pages from the raunchier skin mags—and Nelson recommended them to me affectionately, the way a thesis advisor might recommend outside reading.

In the late afternoons he'd take me Upstairs. Together we'd check the corners for accuracy, Nelson at his surveyor's transit, me acting the part of "rod-man," holding a seven-foot gradated pole to the floor so Nelson could take a reading. We worked in the high forties and fifties, mostly, while four-by-eight-foot panes of plate glass were being blown out of the lower stories and smashing in pieces among pedestrians below.

Rod-man was a profession both simple and demanding. It entailed walking the rod to the very edge of the building, nothing between me and the sky but a single strand of safety cable set at waist height. I was required to stand perfectly still there, holding the rod perfectly upright. And I did that. Only once did I balk at an assignment. There was a tricky corner on the fifty-third floor, a triangular section of concrete and iron that cantilevered out beyond the safety cable and sloped down several inches. "Step out there and give me a read," Nelson said, all lips and gums and watery sad eyes.

I looked out beyond the wire, looked back at him. "Do you want me to?"

He paused, cut off a small smile. "Nah, let me get it." He took the rod and, with a blood-alcohol level somewhere up in the 0.2 range, climbed over the cable, stepped out onto the bare, wind-blown corner, and stood there calmly giving me instructions on how to focus the transit lens and take readings.

Near the beginning of August, one of the ironworkers fell several stories—down a stairwell—and broke an arm and ribs. Rico told me almost no one worked on the iron for more than eight or ten years without slipping up somehow, smashing, a hand or a foot, losing concentration for an instant and falling—through the center of the building much more often than over the side. In his youth, our boss Alex had fallen ten stories down an elevator shaft, landing on his heels and shattering every bone from the soles of his feet to his hips.

A week after the stairwell accident, a two-ton concrete slab fell on an engineer at another job a few blocks down the street, and crushed him to death. The crane had been improperly braced, had started to topple. There had been enough time for the workers to flee, but the engineer had run back to save his transit and ended up losing his life. The man, it turned out, lived not far from me, and I remember riding home on the subway that afternoon wondering whether it was machismo that had killed him, or his attachment to an expensive tool, or just a sense of invincibility, or just fate. I thought about him and his family, about the thin invisible barrier that stood between life and death, and the way different people dealt with that. I was seventeen, and it all seemed fairly distant, someone else's concern. Still, my time Upstairs and the events of that week had stripped me of one layer of the protective film seventeen-year-olds come wrapped in.

On the job site, these two accidents were treated with

a kind of stern, unsentimental respect. The ironworkers were familiar with death and injury. Many of the men drank and whored so as not to have to dwell on such matters, and collected their large paychecks partly in compensation for having to labor in immediate proximity to things most people can easily ignore.

Toward the end of the summer, the crew settled back into its normal routine. One of the ironworkers had a side job as a bookie, and would come into the trailer on coffee break to copy down numbers, collect or pay out small sums of money, or kill time with Rico, who went on grinding out the paychecks week after week. Unlike the other men I had dealings with, Rico was married, and would talk about his wife with some affection. He visited the Combat Zone with the rest of the gang, but told me in private that he drew a different line between what he would and would not do there. Once, I was charged with the duty of driving out into the suburbs to deliver a parcel to his wife. I don't remember what the box contained, or why she had to receive it before the end of the day, but I do remember feeling strange and uneasy meeting her, what with all the stories Rico had told me, what with my virginal notion of the joys and obligations of marriage.

In the last week of my tenure, I was called upon to draft a letter of recommendation for a man I had never met, one of the ironworkers who were so constantly at risk eight hundred feet above us. "The boss needs to have something on paper for this guy," Rico told me. "He's applying for some kind of a position with the head company, see, this guy. And he asked the boss for a recommendation, and the boss isn't that fine with words, so he asked me to ask if you would you do it."

"But I don't know him," I said. "I don't know what to say. What's he like?"

"He's a good guy. You know, you've seen him around. Billy. Just say he's a good guy, add a few fancy words, and it'll be fine."

I was given two sheets of watermarked paper and use of the office typewriter, and within an hour or so I handed over three paragraphs of high praise for Billy and his work, the recommendation littered with two-dollar words, the prose formal and billowing, as if Billy had been an angel instead of an ironworker, as if he were the epitome of masculine perfection. It seemed a harmless enough piece of dishonesty, the least I could do in return for having taken up space in the trailer all summer—and having been paid to do so.

The next morning Alex called me into his office. Though wise in the ways of interpreting architectural plans and managing his ironworkers, he was a crude man, built like a block of stone, with a square head and a blunt little nose and a posture more suitable to the boxing ring than to ordinary civil communication. Over the course of the summer, though we'd worked within a few feet of each other most of every day, he had not sent more than a word or two in my direction, and who could blame him? He was up to his neck in a nightmare of a project, windows blowing out, lawsuits being filed over the flooded basements of nearby hotels, huge penalties about to be waged on the company for every day it fell behind schedule. No doubt he carried the weight of the entire Hancock Tower on his shoulders, on the shattered bones of his legs.

During our ten-week acquaintance, I had not seen him smile nor heard him laugh. He was not laughing or smiling on that day either, but there was a twist of something different in his black eyes. In his hands he held the recommendation I'd written, and he spoke in a quiet, conspiratorial voice. "This," he said, fixing his eyes on me like steel rivets. "You wrote this yourself. This is unbelievable, perfect. This is what education's all about."

I mumbled something I hoped was modest and stoic, and he released me back to the wearisome comfort of my desk. There, secretly pleased, I passed the last few days of the summer undisturbed, then went Upstairs a final time with Nelson, shook hands all around, and left the trailer and the Hancock Tower for a different school.

In the Heart of the Heart of Siberia

In every life there are small events—seemingly small events—that thoroughly alter the direction and shape of what follows them. One little lever is pulled, the tracks are moved a few inches left or right, and the train ends up traveling due east, when it had been headed northwest from its first hour. Instead of staying in Boston on a spring afternoon, you decide, spur of the moment, to make a trip to Providence, and there bump into a young woman you haven't seen since your college days, and never expected to see again, and the woman ends up becoming your wife and bearing your children. Returning home from a trip to the West Coast, you take World Airways flight 815 on a Wednesday, and fly into Boston uneventfully, but the next day flight 815 crash-lands at Logan, skidding into the sea and killing the pilot and two passengers.

It's all the invisible hand of God, you tell yourself, weaving the tapestry of your fate from the fibers of apparent coincidence. Or it's nothing more than the blind careening of a trillion molecules, as random as roulette, meaningless, structureless, pointless. You glue a "Shit Happens" sticker on the bumper of your car. Or you scrape that one off and replace it with "Magic Happens." Or you eschew bumper stickers altogether, and forget about theorems and philosophies and scientific proof and religious doctrine, and just live out the quirky twists of your days minute by minute, hoisting your bundle of good and bad breaks onto your back and walking forward in the direction of the mystery of mysteries.

In the spring of 1967, I was sitting in English class at McKinley Junior High School in Revere, Massachusetts, when a student walked in and handed a note to the teacher. It was a tiny event, the end of a process my parents and I had set in motion a year earlier, and the beginning of something else, another process, another line of tumbling dominoes, that would carry me from Revere to Russia, from the working class to the world.

The teacher silently read the note, thanked the student, and a moment later announced that "someone in our class" had won a half-scholarship to Saint John's Prep, a well-regarded Catholic high school half an hour to the north. The someone was me. I was happy about the news, and at the same time wished the teacher hadn't made a public affair out of it. This was eighth grade, after all: better to be known for almost anything—quick fists, quick wits, an uncle with a nice car—other than academic ambition and good homework habits.

I was accepted to several boarding schools as well, but

since I was such a midget of a boy, immature physically, immature emotionally, my parents thought I should stay at home for another year or two before going away. Saint John's was within commuting distance, and, thanks to the scholarship, affordable; it would make a nice stepping stone between the slippery, rocky shore of public school and the pastures of the rich on the sunny far bank.

Soon a packet arrived, listing my courses, and shifting the rails of my fate a few more degrees farther from Revere and the well-trodden path of family and friends. Geometry, Religion, English, Biology, History, Russian. "Russian?" I said to my parents. "Why did they give me Russian?"

Why were we born in Revere and not Katmandu, I might as well have asked them. Why did you have three boys instead of three girls?

Ruski iazik. From the moment I opened my Russian textbook at the start of the school year at Saint John's I was humbled. Schoolwork had always come so easily to me, and here I was staring dumbly at a crooked alphabet and impenetrable grammar charts—declensions, conjugations—as if I had done nothing but fight, make wise cracks, and ride around in my uncle's Mustang all through grammar school and junior high. *On nichevo nye znayet* was the way they said it over there: He nothing not knows. *Nothing not knows?* I was a logical, stubborn, straight forward type of fourteen-year-old. The idea that there might be such radical differences in the structure of other languages made no sense to me. Why use the forbidden double negative? Why reverse the order of things? Why have one word—*idti*—that meant "to walk" if the walking was being done in a straight line, and a different word—*khadit*—that meant "to walk" if the walking was aimless, a stroll in the park? Why have different endings for all these cases—nominative, genitive, dative, instrumental, accusative, prepositional—when we got along absolutely perfectly well in English without that?

The Russian teacher at Saint John's was a fiery young Soviet woman who, following the trail of her own quirky fate, had married an American and come to Danvers, Massachusetts, to set up home. Early in the semester she became so outraged at the inattentiveness of one of my classmates that she grabbed the pile of textbooks on his desk, marched over to the window, and threw them out. Given my performance in her class, the books could just as easily have been mine. I tried, I struggled, but some sea change had taken place inside me. I had gone from being a confident, outstanding student, to a troubled, mediocre one. I had started making wisecracks in the back of the room. My grades fell from straight A's to low B's, and near the end of the year the assistant principal called me into his office and warned me that I might lose the scholarship if I didn't shape up.

Sophomore year I worked harder, made some A's, managed to keep the scholarship. I applied a second time to the boarding schools, was accepted to most of them again, including Phillips Exeter, grew and matured, and enrolled there as a junior in the fall of 1969. But the pattern repeated itself. Wrenched out of my element again, I floundered academically at first, slipping into the territory of the high C's, and even a D or two, before I slowly righted the ship and graduated with honors. These precipitous dips in the graph of my scholastic achievement were a puzzle to my parents and teachers, but it is clear to me now that I was trying to reorder my interior world to suit the exterior changes. Somewhere in the mixed-up middle of me, I was trying to make sense of the fact that people lived as differently as they did, trying to hold tight to the commandments of my upbringing—toughness, self-sacrifice, loyalty, family before all—in the face of the sudden understanding that there were other ways to think and be, other grammars of the human condition.

Learning has as much to do with emotion as with aptitude, and in those confusing years, like many adolescents, I could never quite clear my emotional slate enough to sustain the discipline I needed to be a diligent student. As if to make up for my time as the short, brainy, teacher-pleaser in McKinley Junior High, I focused on friendships at Exeter and on sports (baseball, cross-country, hockey, rowing). Instead of putting in the extra work necessary for taking hold of the rules of calculus and Russian once and for all, I did what I absolutely had to do and little more. I was consumed by the onset of an inner revolution that was as potent, in its own tiny arena, as anything St. Petersburg saw in 1917. I was wriggling free of the blanket of rules in which I had been swaddled since birth, a blanket cut from the rough wool of working-class life, woven from threads of presumed superiority and nagging insecurity, financial unpredictability of the highest order, and the guaranteed presence of warm and obvious affection.

My parents sent me to Exeter so I could get into Harvard, so I could make a lucrative career out of my braininess, so I could have what they and their neighbors did not have: a new car; a summer home; all the confidence, social ease, and freedom from worry enjoyed by people in the fancier suburbs.

But the message I had been given all my life was that the inhabitants of the fancier suburbs thought too much of themselves. They looked down on people like us, and were not truly happy or at peace, in spite of their tennis clubs and silverware. Somehow, I was supposed to go to Exeter, and Harvard, build a career in some prestigious profession, own a large house on several acres near the country club, and remain exactly who I was. The impossibility of that expectation, the weight of it, sat upon my academic life like a load of stone in a kid's red wagon.

I didn't get into Harvard—or Brown, or Dartmouth, or Cornell—and, the fall after my Hancock Tower summer, started college at Boston University, a perfectly fine school where there were plenty of working-class kids and where, for some reason known only to God, I continued studying Russian. My professor there was a kindly, elderly émigré with white hair rolled into a bun on top of her head. One afternoon she took me aside and said, "You are a smart boy, I know you are. Why aren't you working the way you should be working?"

She would have had to live another thirty years to hear an intelligent answer to that question.

But, repeating the odd pattern I'd designed for myself in high school, the next term I worked a bit harder. I applied to Brown, was admitted as a junior transfer, and continued my battles with conjugations and declensions there, making a little progress and ending up, senior year, earning a solid B. I still had no idea what I wanted to do with my life. Be a doctor, my parents suggested, a diplomat, a professor. But it did not really matter what they suggested because some larger force—invisible, unstoppable—was pushing me steadily along in the direction of things Russian.

Despite my troubles with the language, I was a good literature student. From the moment I read the first few pages of Dostoevsky's *Notes from Underground*, I felt as if the prose of Russia's Golden Age had been written with people like me in mind. There were familiar class tensions, and the continual tug of guilt and obligation that accompanies a serious religious life. There were provincial boys plucked out of their element and dropped into the sophisticated swirl of the Moscow elite. There were sons rebelling against their parents' traditions, there were priests and criminals, saints, brainy booklovers, and men who could sometimes not bring themselves to climb out of bed. I felt closer to Konstantin Levin than to Joey Brandano down the block. Turgenev, Leskov, Tolstoy, Chekhov, Goncharov—the world they depicted made immediate sense to me, as if I had lived there in another incarnation.

But if I had lived there in another incarnation, why couldn't I master the language? Eight years of study, and I could barely understand the literature I loved when I tried to read it in the original. Wanting to spend another year close to my girlfriend, I stayed at Brown two more terms and earned a master's degree, making all A's again, as if to remind myself of the person I'd been in junior high. During that year a professor told me about a program run by the U.S. State Department, a government-to-government cultural exchange that sent large traveling exhibits to the Soviet Union. It was the best way to spend time in that country without paying to do so, she said, and spending time there was the best way to really learn the language.

I applied, was accepted, and in the winter of 1977, along with twenty-four other Russian-speaking Americans, went to Washington, D.C., for a month of training before being shipped out. Those weeks were not without their anxieties. Perhaps hoping I would change my mind about leaving, my girlfriend gave me the memoir of an American man named Alexander Dolgun, who'd been stationed at the embassy in Moscow, and who, in 1946, had been kidnapped and tortured (the KGB operatives did not allow him to sleep, they beat the bottoms of his feet with clubs) then sent to the gulag for seven years. And, near the end of training, as if to back her up, members of the USIA security service locked us in a windowless room on Pennsylvania Avenue and frightened us with the tale of a married American diplomat who'd been seduced by a gorgeous blonde KGB agent. Secret cameras had been hidden in the wall outlets of the blonde's bedroom, and as the diplomat was walking to work the next week, a man jumped out of the bushes and showed him very clear photographs of himself and the blonde *in flagrante delicto*. "Compromised" was the word the USIA security officers used. The KGB will try to compromise you. Never go out alone with Soviet citizens. Always assume your hotel telephone is bugged. Never tell anyone what you see inside the American Embassy. Never sign your name to any document, no matter how harmless it seems.

By the end of that briefing I was so afraid of being compromised and sent back to Revere in disgrace that when I stepped out into the Washington winter day and a pan-handler approached me, I suspected—this is absolutely true—that he might be an agent of the communist demons.

But, at the end of training, my new friends and I, all uncompromised at this point, were put on a Swissair flight to Moscow. Except for two short car trips to Canada, I had never been outside the United States. Except for a quick flight to New York City as part of our training, I had never been on a commercial airplane. The span of the dark Atlantic, the green and black farmland outside Zurich, the strong coffee and strange coins in the airport cafeteria there—all of it was thrilling and exotic. The name of the Moscow airport—Sheremetevo – the echoing, incomprehensible announcements in the mother tongue, the stern faces of the Border Guards as they spent such a long time studying the photos on our passports, the fact that, as, we watched, an employee of the American Embassy smoothed our passage through Customs with a bribe of two bottles of vodka—all of it, was exceedingly strange and wonderful and edged with a fine lining of fear.

On that first evening we boarded a chartered bus at twilight and made the hour-long drive from Sheremetevo into the thousand-year-old capital, and it was like flying very slowly through the dark, mysterious reaches of the atmosphere of Saturn or Mars. Tilted log houses lined the road, buried to the knees in the frozen dirt. Women in kerchiefs and black boots struggled along in the snow carrying shopping bags in both bare hands. Grandfathers stumbled behind them, stupefied with alcohol. Cars—un-American cars, small and tinny—trundled past in the opposite lane with men in fur hats at the wheel.

By the time we'd covered ten miles, a cold Russian darkness had fallen over the highway, and the log cabins had given way to rows of shoddy concrete apartment buildings, lookalike claptraps with uneven rooflines and slogans hung in large letters between floors. *Glory to the People and the Party! Forward to the Victory of Communism! Lenin Lived, Lives, and Will Live! Let There Always Be Sunshine! Communism Equals Soviet Power Plus Electrification of the Whole Land!*

Let there always be sunshine? What kind of a bizarre civilization had I landed in—nuclear missiles, log houses straight out of the eighteenth century, and Let There Always Be Sunshine? Cars bumping and sputtering along dark roads with only their parking lights showing, the streetlamps frail and flickering, the storefronts absolutely plain and unadorned, with generic signs over the front doors—Bakery, Fruits and Vegetables, Meat. It was a drab, rough, secret world, and it sounded a sweet and strangely familiar tune in my bones.

The bus turned into Red Square. As we were offered a glimpse of Saint Basil's with its twirling onion domes, then the red brick face of the Kremlin, every cold war cliché rose up around me. Tanks and missile launchers on May Day. KGB torturers and dirty tricks. Drunkenness, ugliness, enforced atheism. They would hate us, these people. What were we doing here?

What we were doing there was trying to convince them to live like us.

During the cold war, the United States Information Agency—an arm of the Department of State—crossed the Iron Curtain with Voice of America radio broadcasts, and traveling exhibitions like the one on which I served. (It was at the first of these exhibits, in Moscow, that Nikita Khrushchev and Richard Nixon held their famous "kitchen debate," arguing about the relative merits of two antagonistic political systems.) Each exhibition focused on one aspect of American life—agriculture, computer technology, design—and was sent, with its American staff, to major cities like Moscow, Leningrad, and Kiev, as well as to lesser known provincial centers like Irkutsk, Novosibirsk, Donetsk, Tashkent, and Tbilisi. Twenty-five Russian-speaking American guides manned the show. Those guides, a few non-Russian-speaking technical specialists, and an administrative staff of eight other Americans would arrive in a city with their luggage and thirty freight containers filled with exhibit material, and for the next two-and-a-half weeks they'd work long hours setting up the displays in a rented pavilion. When everything was in place, there would be a fancy official opening featuring the American Ambassador and some local Party apparatchiks. And then the doors would be thrown wide and the public would stream in. There was no admission fee. It was not uncommon to see the line outside the exhibit's front door stretching more than a mile—in snowstorms and hail, in blistering heat. Soviet citizens—all kinds of Soviet citizens, powerful and powerless, radical and conservative, good communists and veterans of the prison camps, students and collective farmers, men who'd fought the Nazis and women who'd been sentenced to psychological hospitals for their political beliefs—would pour into the brightly lit patch of Americana at the astonishing rate of fifteen thousand per day. Desperate for convertible currency as they were, the Soviet leaders allowed these little bubbles of capitalist propaganda onto their soil in exchange for absurdly high rent payments for everything from the buildings where the exhibits were housed to the abandoned parking lots where our containers were parked. They then tried every trick they could think of —snide newspaper reviews, harassment by paid provocateurs, a large police presence, bureaucratic delays—to keep the Americans from doing what they had been sent there to do.

The title of the 1977 exhibit was "Photography USA," and the ten-thousand-square-foot show included the new SX-70 camera; a circular auditorium into which a hundred people could squeeze, and on the walls of which, to the continuous accompaniment of John Denver music, flashed somewhat idealized images of American life: the Golden Gate Bridge, Wisconsin farmhouses, the Manhattan skyline, etc.; a softly lit gallery of Stieglitz and Eisenstaedt portraits; curved walls covered with snapshots from the cameras of ordinary American families; a darkroom with special glass and lights so passing visitors could watch American photographers at work; a functioning portrait studio; an expensive camera/telescope used for photographing stars (this was stolen at the end of the tour, in the last city); several hundred smaller displays. All this would be shown to the citizens of a country that did not have dental floss, unleaded gasoline, or—except for a brief period in the fall—fresh vegetables in its stores.

But my fellow guides and I saw none of those displays until we left the capital. After a day or two of briefings at the Moscow embassy, we were put on an Aeroflot plane and flown 500 miles east to the city of Ufa, where our containers waited on a dreary, expensive patch of asphalt in a park. Ufa was a ruined vision out of the last century, an industrial town of 900,000 in the foothills of the Urals. You could still see horse-drawn wagons trundling down the main street loaded with metal milk cans. And the corner market a few hundred yards from our hotel offered only sacks of old flour, blocks of unappetizing white cheese, stale candy; perhaps, on special days, a stringy chicken or two and a fatty, gristly piece of lamb for which dozens of people would be waiting in line. After we'd settled into our hotel and established a work routine, my American colleagues and I would walk down to that store after dinner—for lack of anything else to do—and spend a portions of our food allowance on hard, tasteless cookies, or a little sugar for tea. When we stepped back out into the night, children would surround us like hungry, urchins, yelling *"Zvachka! Zvachka!"* *Gum! Gum!* and spouting, in heavy accents, a phrase or two of English from their junior high school texts: "Mai naime ees Yuri. Vat ees yur naime?"

In the first week of March, Ufa was a cold wasteland, devoid of beauty, quintessentially Soviet: packed, clacking trolleys in the road, huge statues of Lenin in the park. We ate breakfast in the hotel cafeteria where the offerings were limited to horsemeat goulash, potato salad, champagne, and under boiled hot dogs served with a few peas and washed down with a kind of sourish liquid yogurt said to be excellent for digestion.

My job, and the job of the twenty-four other guides, was to stand on the exhibit floor and answer questions in Russian, six hours a day, six days a week "How much does a loaf of bread cost in America?" one of the visitors would ask.

"That depends," you'd say. *Zavisit.*

Zavisit ot chevo? "Depends on what? How can it depend?"

"Depends on the type of bread, where in America it's being sold, whether it's in a supermarket or a small corner store, whether or not it's on sale that day."

"Hmph. Here, we always know what bread costs. Go to Vladivostok, go to Murmansk, always the same. Bread is twenty-two kopeks."

At this whiff of controversy, a small crowd would gather, pressing three-deep in a tight half circle around the guide, soaking him or her in streams of pent-up curiosity. The questions would follow each other like raindrops in a downpour, and the subject would skip from bread to meat to race relations to Vietnam to rock music to the fine points of the rules of baseball or the Electoral College.

Always, in our visitors' voices, we could hear echoes of the confident bitterness of Soviet propaganda. Often, the questioner's tone held a mix of superiority and insecurity—instantly familiar to me from my younger days. *Oo nas luchshye*, they would tell us. We have it better. Though the men and women making such assertions had never been beyond the borders of their own country, never seen anything but government-controlled TV, in most cases never even spoken with someone who'd passed an hour in Paris, or a weekend in New York. Why can't black and white people sit at the same table in America, they would ask. Why are your police always beating students? You say you have fresh fruit all year long but that's because you're a child of wealthy capitalists, isn't it? Otherwise, how could you have gotten this job? Why is your government so aggressive? Why did you drop the atomic bomb on Japan?

It was an advanced course in the Russian language, and an eight-month graduate seminar in human psychology, as well. Not only because we saw how easily masses of people could be lied to and terrorized, but because we encountered, at close range, evil-faced KGB provocateurs and closed-minded communists, stupid people spouting shibboleths, brainy adolescents trying to be cool, and great numbers of brave, ordinary, warmhearted men and women who were able to see through our propaganda and their own and speak to us humbly and directly, unarmored, as if we were just human beings, people whom fate—a small turn at some point in the soul's karmic travels—had landed in Boston rather than Byelorus.

After our second week of work, one of the other

guides told me he'd heard there was a mosque in Ufa, on the outskirts of town. Something local and offbeat and real, a threat to the atheistic Leninist monolith. On our day off we boarded a city bus and made the mistake of asking the driver if this was the route that would take us past the mosque.

He nodded tersely and looked at us out of the sides of his eyes. A few minutes later the bus pulled to the curb, and all the passengers were told to get off. All the passengers, that is, except for me and my friend, and two leather-jacketed fellows who'd taken the seat in front of us. None of the passengers complained too loudly. Everybody off the bus, period, right here in the middle of the route. The doors closed and we were driven to the mosque, a small white-clapboarded chapel on a rise, conveniently locked up. Our leather-jacketed friends acted as tour guides, said we were welcome to take pictures of the building, but not of them. When we'd seen enough, they put us on the bus again and drove us back to the hotel.

On May Day, almost at the end of our tenure in Ufa, everyone on the exhibit staff was extended the honor of being invited onto the reviewing platform for the big parade. We accepted, of course, and stood for four hours behind Party officials in East German–made topcoats who raised gloved hands at the marching soldiers and cart-wheeling gymnasts below. All the while a crude public address system blared out tape recorded messages: "Hail Comrade Brezhnev! Glory to the Great Socialist Worker's State!" at earsplitting volume. The parade was a bizarre mix of cynicism and innocence—second-graders in pigtails and school uniforms waving to the famous men on stage, and factory workers shuffling along in boots, making crude remarks beneath their breath, waiting to be released to the drunken pleasures of the holiday afternoon.

I had made, one friend in Ufa, a young man named Roman. Roman was a student at the agricultural college, and he would come to the hotel sometimes at night and we'd sit on chairs in the lobby and play chess. I'd made friends with him, I think, because of his utter guilelessness. He was the simplest of country boys, living with his grandmother, studying agronomy, innocent, naive, not a political bone in his body. After the parade, in flagrant violation of the no-going-out-with-Soviets-alone rule, I rode an impossibly crowded bus into the countryside with Roman and a half-dozen of his friends and we had a picnic in a field there, surrounded by hardwood forests just blossoming. No one asked me the price of bread in America. No one pressed me to explain my government's involvement in Vietnam. No one wanted to know whether or not it was true that we were planning to use the neutron bomb against selected cities in Eastern Europe.

We built a fire on the shore of a two-acre pond, grilled shish-kabob on green twigs, baked potatoes in the coals and drank absurd amounts of vodka, Russian-style, straight-up. Someone had brought along a guitar, and Roman and his friends sang army songs, school songs, and sentimental Russian ballads, and long after dark we sobered up enough to find our way back to the road and hitch a ride to the city in an army jeep, driven by a major in uniform who said absolutely nothing to us during the entire trip.

Roman was a part of the Soviet Union that the USIA security men had not told us about. In the midst of such a nation—teetering along toward economic collapse, built on lies and genocide, infested with the most horrific national insecurity complex imaginable—in the midst of that was preserved, by some miracle, an innocence as pure and humble as anything Eden ever saw. It is part of the Russian national character, that innocence. It accounts, perhaps, for the ability of so many of its people to believe such obvious lies for so long. It accounts for the country's history of beloved, bloodthirsty tyrants, for its religious devotion, its tolerance of corruption, perhaps for its great artistic achievements, as well.

In the USSR I came face-to-face with thieves, torturers, professional liars and leg breakers, the worst kind of cowardice and deceit. But running through all that like a pure flute note was this beautiful Russianness, this ability to find the route into the tenderest, most intimate reaches of another human soul and remain there. The capacity for a kind of friendship you are hard pressed to find anywhere else on earth. It was a shock to me, that tenderness, after years of American news reports about the communist demon, and after the cantankerous give-and-take of the exhibit floor. It was a lesson like the lessons I had learned when I left my neighborhood: that fear wears the most convincing disguises, that we manufacture—myth by myth, injury upon injury—an armor of assumptions about the rest of humanity. We create an unsavory *them* — communists or liberals, men, women, the rich, the Irish,

the Jews, the Republicans, the blacks, the whites, the Mex-
icans—because it tricks us into believing we have an *us*.
The *us* is better, of course; people go their whole lives believing in the righteousness of that *us*. It's not easy to slip
free of such a comfortable shell. Out in the cold air again,
you feel raw and vulnerable, you're tempted to find a new
myth to fold over yourself, something more sophisticated;
you're anxious to create a new *them*.

But a case can be made that the apparent coincidences
of human life are continuously nudging the individual
forward, into the territory of a new grammar, a larger and
larger *us*. What's asked of us is the courage to take other
people as they are, without labeling them; to leave the familiar comforts of habit and opinion and open ourselves
to actual experience. Perhaps this is the "childlike" state
mentioned in the Bible, the "beginner's mind" Zen masters talk about and point their disciples toward. Living that
way, unarmored, has nothing to do with leaving the
neighborhood and traveling abroad—those are external
changes, mere decoration. You can climb all the rungs of
the socioeconomic ladder, walk on the shores of all the
continents, and remain as tightly closed-up as ever. Or you
can spend your whole life in Revere, or Utah, or Blago-
veshchensk, and still find that open territory. Here were
these Soviet citizens, after all, corralled and lied to, and
welcoming Americans into their houses night after night
as if we were family. Here was an army major, in uniform,
taking a bunch of drunk twenty-somethings off a dark
road and driving us back to his drab, suffering city.

From Ufa, we shipped our containers and suitcases

four thousand miles east to the city of Novosibirsk and set up shop there in a sweltering geodesic dome. Strange to be sweating all day in Siberia. But it was June by the time the show opened, the days were humid and long, and after work we still had six hours of daylight for our explorations. Ili Novosibirsk, too, we were followed and harassed. On one early summer evening a co-worker and I rode the commuter train fifteen miles out into the Siberian wilderness and got off at a dirt-road hamlet called Krakhal, intending to walk around, take a picture or two, perhaps strike up a new acquaintance or find a cafe that served tea and dumplings. A KGB flunkey had followed us from the city. Pretending to be drunk, he jumped off the train and trailed us into the woods, began harassing us as we walked. "Hey, wha you doin' here? Hey. Lishen to me. *Slushai, slushai*" After a minute or two of this, he put a hand on my friend's shoulder and I grabbed his wrist and roughly flung it off. Immediately two deputized peace-keepers—sturdy young fellows wearing the telltale red armbands—appeared out of the trees and escorted us back to the train station.

Everyone—customers, ticket clerks—was cleared out. The doors were bolted. I and my friend, who did not speak Russian, were herded into one corner of the wood-walled room and battered with questions: What were our names? Why were we there, in the hamlet of Krakhal? Where did we live in America? What had we taken pictures of? The two deputies did the interrogating, and, from time to time, the pretend-drunk, a tall, mean-looking man in his early thirties, would become infuriated by our answers and rush at us as if he were about to take a swing. After the fourth or fifth of these made-up rages, I could no longer stand the tension. I stepped straight at him, pointed, shouted *Khvatit! Enough!*, spouted a few curse words in English, used all the old street tricks I could think of. And he snarled at me, smirked, slouched back onto his bench on the far side of the room and fell silent.

The interrogation went on for thirty minutes. When it was over we were, presented with a one-page, handwritten document and asked to sign our names. I read it over carefully, grateful that three months of constant conversation had improved my Russian to the point where I could understand every word. Nothing our interrogators had written down was untrue. It was a neutral stating of facts, an account of everything we had just said. I could see no reason not to sign it. I translated it for my friend; he had no problem with it either—anything to get us out of that building. One of the interrogators handed me a pen. And just at that, moment I remembered the briefing in the windowless room in Washington, the security agents' faces, their urgent tone, their paranoia.

"We can't sign this," I said to one of the red-armbanded men. "*Nye mozhem podpisat.*"

The drunk stirred in a menacing way.

"You can't sign the *Akt?*"

"No. I'm sorry, we can't."

"But it's all true, isn't it Everything there is just what you told us."

"Right. But we're not allowed to sign any document of any kind."

"You refuse to sign the *Akt?*"

"*Da.*"

There was a terrible pause, surely the most awful empty moment I've ever lived through. The three men glared at us. We looked back at them, looked away, waited. I could feel my heart banging in my chest. My friend, a photography specialist, was shaking like a poplar leaf in a gale.

"Then take the last train back to the city and never come here again," the more brazen of our interrogators said.

"When is the last train?"

"Ten minutes. Never come here again."

The doors were unlocked and we were let out of the depot building. We made a loop around it on a dirt track, trying to calm ourselves, not risking a snapshot or a word or a glance back over our shoulders. When the last train to Novosibirsk rolled in, we were waiting on the platform.

During those summer months in Novosibirsk, I made two very good friends: an eighteen-year-old young woman named Tanya, and a twenty-six-year-old young man named Tolya. Tolya worked at the exhibit as an electrician's apprentice, and by the end of the two-week construction period we had already grown close. Our friendship consisted of evening walks through the streets of the city (wide, paved boulevards, almost empty of traffic; four- and five-story stone buildings in the center, surrounded by a ring of ugly apartment houses, surrounded by a ring of log cabins, surrounded by Siberian forest and tundra) and cups of tea, conversations about books and women, religion, willpower, yoga and vegetarianism, Jesus and Schweitzer, the purpose of life. Tolya had been paralyzed as a teenager after a wrestling accident, told he'd never move again outside his wheelchair, but had willed himself to heal, just as he now willed himself to survive, psychologically, in an environment that oppressed him. The environment in which I'd grown up had been nothing like his, not oppressive, not filled with lies, not watched over by sadistic policemen and their red-armbanded lackeys. But there was a way in which I'd strained against the boundaries of it, too, a way in which I was still trying, by the force of my will, to free myself of old expectations and injuries and stand up and walk into a freer, truer self Tolya and I were tied together by a kind of ambition that had nothing to do with new cars and summer homes.

In every city there were KGB agents assigned to the exhibit building, disguised as pavilion executives. We became expert at sorting them out from the run-of-the-mill functionaries, and avoiding them. In Novosibirsk, the agent was a young, athletic, particularly nasty man by the name of Nikolai, who wore a gray suit and an open collared shirt and sniffed around us making snide remarks as we worked.

"Nikolai is, trying to keep me from seeing you," Tolya told me after a couple of weeks. "He said to me yesterday: When your American pal leaves we are going to beat you and beat you so that you'll wish for us to kill you."

On our last walk he said, "If I write you a letter saying my mother is ill it means I want to leave the country. Will you help me come to America?"

I promised to do that. I ripped a dollar in two and gave him one half He ripped a ruble in two and gave me one half as a parting gift, I presented him with a paperback copy of *Don Quixote*, and then wrote him letter after letter when I returned home. All of them went unanswered. I asked a friend in Novosibirsk to go to Tolya's house and inquire about him. She did, and wrote this: "I went to the address you sent me, and found Tolya's family. He no longer lives in Novosibirsk. The family would not tell me where he is now, they say they do not want any contact with foreigners." In 1993 I published a novel set in the Soviet Union, and dedicated it to Tolya, hoping against hope that the book would be translated into Russian, and he would see the dedication, and perhaps write and say that his mother was ill. But there is only silence now in the territory once occupied by that friendship. No doubt Nikolai and his pals arrested and beat him, bothered his parents and friends at work, pressed him for information about me, perhaps sent him to jail or to the camps as an example to others who might befriend visiting Americans. That was what the KGB agents believed to be their true purpose in life, keeping the impure capitalist *them* from tainting their Marxist-Leninist *us*, keeping the psychological boundaries in place, maintaining the paralysis of the status quo, as if they were the physical manifestation of what, for most of us, are internal, less visible, but equally limiting barriers.

The KGB operatives were a clumsy, closed-minded, sadistic bunch—at least at our low level. They'd invite a few of us into their offices for a drink after work, wait until we'd had a glass or two of vodka, and then suggest a trip to a whorehouse. They'd listen in on our conversations on the exhibit floor and, later, interrogate visitors who'd dared to make less than positive comments about the USSR.

They'd follow us around the city, clumsily, stupidly, or with a tough-guy arrogance. It was annoying, infuriating, amusing—and nothing at all compared to what they did to their own people, often to the best of their own people. In the West, we had this image of the KGB as composed of sophisticated spies and assassins, and at higher levels that's what they were. But at the middle and lower levels, in the provinces, they were just thugs, dumb fucks—torturers in some cases, brainwashed country boys in others—paid to maintain and promulgate the rampant insecurities of their leaders, paid to keep the armor in place. *Komityet Gosudarstvenni Bezapastnosti* was what the acronym stood for: The Committee of Government Safety.

But Tanya, like Tolya, would not be intimidated by them. She came into the exhibit one day, waited until the crowd around me had dispersed, then walked up and said, "Do you want to go on a date?"

"A date?" I said, thinking that perhaps *svidaniya* had another meaning I was not aware of

"Yes. A date. With me."

"Sure," I said.

"Do you know the cafe behind the opera theater? I'll meet you there at eight o'clock."

"Sure, fine. I'll see you there at eight. *Uvidimsya tam v vosem.*"

I was certain she was a KGB plant, but I wanted to see her anyway. If I had to be compromised, it wouldn't be such a terrible thing to have the compromising done by a beautiful young woman. I had no state secrets to leak. The worst that could happen was I'd be sent home . . . and after five months without fresh vegetables, that didn't exactly seem like the harshest of punishments. Before going out to meet her that evening, I told some of my friends that if I wasn't back by midnight they should alert the exhibit director and come looking for me.

But it took me only a minute or so in her company to understand that Tanya wasn't the type to be hiding cameras in her wall outlets. She was a *chista Sibirianka*, a pure Siberian, with a hundred-year pedigree in those parts— blonde as blonde, with large blue eyes and a large mouth and prominent cheekbones. I cannot explain what attracted her to me—perhaps she'd been listening at the edge of the conversation and had liked something I'd said. And I can't say exactly what attracted me to her. Part of it was physical, no doubt. But there was something else as well, something apparent from the first few words of conversation, a certain ease, a certain intuitive mutual understanding one usually finds in relationships of long standing.

We had a nice meal at the cafe that evening—beef Stroganoff, bread and tea; she refused to let me pick up her half of the tab—then walked along the wide boulevards in the warm twilight. She told me she wanted to see me again but did not want me contacting her at home; it wasn't safe even for her to call for me at the hotel, so we arranged another meeting, had another meal, took another walk. She made me a gift of a book of Pushkin's poetry. We began to see each other regularly, each of us bringing something for a picnic—a loaf of bread, cheese, pieces of Russian salami, nuts, dried fruit, cans of Pepsi from the exhibit supply. We'd walk down to the Ob River and catch a commuter hydrofoil, ride out to one of the small uninhabited islands and build a fire there on the beach. We'd kiss and talk, take a swim if the night was warm. Because I had once heard her refer to Lenin as "uncle," and because she had once asked me if living in America was like being in prison, and because the last thing I wanted was to replay the charged discussions of my working day, I steered our conversations away from things political, from comparisons, from the ways in which we were so different.

One night the kissing, talking, and swimming went on so late that we missed the last boat back to the city. We stood there on the bank, in the vast darkness, the personal suddenly turned political, in spite of our best efforts to the contrary. "This is very bad," she said. "My mother will think it is very bad if I don't come home all night."

"And my boss," I said.

And the people at the American Embassy in Moscow, I thought.

After a quarter of an hour spent pacing the dock, we heard the clack and thump of oars in oarlocks, and saw a small boat pushing against the current not far from shore.

"Boys!" Tanya called out across the water. "Help us! We're stranded!"

"We can't, girl," a voice came back. "We can barely

make headway against the current as it is."

"Boys! Help me, please! My mother will be home worrying. You must help me."

"We can't. *Nye mozhem.*

"Boys! please!"

After another exchange or two, the boys—three young men in a skiff—turned their boat around and rowed toward us. "Say nothing, not a word," Tanya whispered to me as we watched them approach. "Your accent will give you away." One of the young men bore an eerie resemblance to Robert Kennedy. One of his oars was a two-by-four. He heaved against them, veins bulging in his throat and forehead, breath coming in gasps. The river was as black as pitch and hundreds of yards wide at that point, and the current was strong. We had no bow light, no light of any kind. He heaved and strained and yard by yard pulled us across the shipping channel and to the far shore.

"Should I offer him some money?" I whispered to Tanya when we climbed out, and she took offense, making a face, turning away. Such an American thing to do, she seemed to be telling me, reducing everything to a business transaction. "Help them pull the boat up onto the sand, that's all."

We kissed good night on a tree-lined street. She caught a late bus home, and I walked to the hotel, where a pensioner slept in the lobby, guarding the locked doors. He let me in, and I climbed back up to my room and lay awake for a long while, wrapped up in the warmth of my feelings for Tanya, listening to the last trolleys stopping in front of the hotel, the twang and snap of their wires, the irregular putter of a Lada or two plying the Siberian night.

Tanya was eighteen and fatherless, studying to become a civil engineer. She never invited me to her home, never admitted to her mother that her new boyfriend was an American. Our nights together on the Ob were so fine and calm, our connection so immediate and whole, that for a time I thought of marrying her, even of staying in Siberia and making some kind of odd expatriate life for myself there because I knew she would never leave that place. It was a crazy idea, a lover's daydream, but I held on to it for a while, making up a fantasy life while I demonstrated the SX-70 to knots of Young Communist League members with smirks on their faces.

Near the end of my time in Novosibirsk, though she was not religious, Tanya took me to a working church, and afterwards presented me with a bronze icon that still hangs next to my desk. The gift must have cost her a week's pay, and would have cost me more if I'd been caught taking it out of the country. It was another risk for her, but she came to the hotel dining room on the last night; we had dinner there then walked out into the park behind and kissed and held each other for a long time. When I said good-bye finally, and pulled myself away, she doubled over as if someone had punched her in the stomach, and let out small moans of grief, and I made myself turn and walk back into the building and up to my room to pack.

Something broke open in me then, the seed pod of my Revere identity, my American self. It was as if, having come to feel what I felt for Tanya and Tolya, I had come to understand—viscerally, not intellectually—that there was a layer of human interaction so much more essential than politics and economics; that all my theories about the superiority of capitalism and democracy were surface decorations, and that something vast and profound lay beneath them. It was certainly true what the American press had told me about communism, about life in the USSR. But it was only one-quarter of the truth. The other three-quarters lay enfolded in the mystery of the human predicament. Next to that universality, that oneness, the visible world with its wars and bad politics seemed somehow beside the point.

I began to question everything I had been told in my life, tapping a hammer to the foundation of the house of my assumptions, checking for holes, weak spots, soft powdery lies. Not because I was flirting with communism I'd seen enough of it to be put off from the idea forever. But because I was beginning to sense that the truth was going to be found in places other than where I'd expected to find it, in the deep murky reaches of the interior world rather than in titles, philosophies, and categories. I turned my back then on the idea of becoming a diplomat, a professor, a doctor, and replaced it with a different sort of ambition: I wanted to find out who I actually was beneath the layers of identity I'd been wearing since I was old enough to speak. I wanted not merely to have a nice title and a pretty wife and plenty of money, but to find my real voice, my true purpose.

In early August, after a vacation on the Black Sea, my fellow guides and I met the "Photography USA" containers in Moscow and set up the show a last time, in Luzhni-ki Park. We were exhausted now by life in the USSR, the same questions again and again, the lack of food we liked, the lack of privacy, the lack of any kind of civility on the streets or business sense in the shops. I dated another Soviet woman, briefly, and went on outings with my American friends—to the parks, to receptions at the Ambassador's house—but Tanya and Tolya had turned the world upside down for me, and I spent most of my time alone. I read Erich Fromm's *Art of Loving*, and Ram Dass's *The Only Dance There Is*—books I once would have scoffed at as being outside the hard, sure realm of the practical and logical. But now they seemed to be pointing toward the door of an unvisited room, a new layer of life that had opened itself up for me. There are no good words for that place. Different people move into it on different vehicles: the self-sacrifice of raising children; the discipline of sports, business, or a religious calling; the required compromises of relationship. For some it comes into view only after a period of solitude, or through the effort of artistic endeavor, or the suffering of a chronic illness. There are no good words for it.

At the end of *A Way of Yaqui Knowledge*, after a series of bizarre exercises assigned by his shaman, Carlos Castaneda says simply, "And then I was alone." That interior solitude was what I had glimpsed and what I was seeking. It seems to me now that it is a foundation without weak spots, the basis for an appreciation of the mystery of being alive. It is the beginning of taking nothing for granted, nothing at someone else's word. It is the prerequisite for love of self, which is the prerequisite for love of anyone else, and I tasted it—just began to taste it—there, of all places, close to the geographical center of the Evil Empire. The memory of that first taste would bring me back to the USSR in 1987 and 1990 for two more extended tours.

We packed up "Photography USA" in late September, just as the first snowflakes were falling on Moscow. After some traveling in Scandinavia and Europe, I returned to America and soon moved out of my parents' house, away from the warmth and security of Revere. Lugging my college degrees and world travels, I went and lived in an unfurnished apartment in the poorest part of Rutland, Vermont, making sandwiches, part-time, in the mountaintop kitchen of a ski resort, taking long solitary walks after work in temperatures that reached twenty-five degrees below zero; reading, thinking, writing poetry, pondering the nature of things. It was, on the surface, an unproductive time. But those months in Rutland were the start of my exploration of a larger life, the life my parents had prepared me for, with their sacrifices and their encouragement and their passed-on ambition for a better place, a richer way. Though explaining that to them was never easy in those days, even in the grammar of the language we all shared.

On Failure

I volunteered for the Peace Corps with one thing in mind: I wanted to help people. In those days, in spite of the fact that my Russian travels had released me from certain assumptions about human difference, I still saw the world as divided neatly into two camps: rich and happy; poor and miserable. Almost everyone in America fell into the first category. We had shelter, food, and basic medical care, while millions of Somalis and Bangladeshis went hungry, unsheltered, untreated. I had sense enough to see that I wouldn't be able to devote my whole life to fixing this imbalance; I wasn't that selfless, that good. But it seemed reasonable to set aside the pursuit of my own happiness for a time, go into the Third World, as it was called then, and dig wells so people could drink, or offer some basic medical treatment so they would not have to endure so much pain, or teach farmers how to better manage their crops so there would be less chance of their children going hungry.

The fact that I had no skills as well-digger, doctor, or

farmer did not worry me. The Peace Corps would provide training, I was sure of that, and then it would be just a matter of enduring, for a couple of years, the discomfort of living in a foreign culture, eating different food, learning another language. What was the worst that could happen?

A twenty-five-year-old's idealism is a wonderful thing. It files down the uneven edges of the world, ignores the mixed motivations, the contradictions, the bitter unsolvable puzzles; it renders life clear, smooth, and holdable. For two years I would give up my spoiled and pampered ways and thereby bring a measure of happiness to the sweaty side of the globe. What could be more obviously good and right?

I signed up to go to Micronesia, a place I thought I'd heard of, but couldn't easily locate on a map. Living briefly with my parents again after my Rutland adventure, I went through the tedious medical exams, had my fingerprints recorded at the local police station (where a cranky lieutenant tried to talk me out of going: "Help your own people first," he said, and I lumped him immediately with the rest of the selfish bourgeoisie, all my narrow-minded compatriots who ate steak and lobster and complained about high taxes). Someone from the Washington office called and warned: "We just want to be sure you know that, along with Nepal, Micronesia has the highest dropout rate in the world for Peace Corps volunteers, 50 percent. Are you sure you want to go there?"

I was sure. I wanted the toughest assignment I could find; I wanted to do the most good. At the end of June I hugged my parents, kissed Amanda—a new girlfriend then—good-bye, and climbed on a plane. Three days of briefings and talks in Los Angeles, three weeks of classes and training in Guam, and the Micronesia contingent was broken up into groups that corresponded to the various districts of that vast territory—Truk, Ponape, Marshalls, Palau, Yap, Kosrae—and sent off for more training, nearer to the areas of our eventual assignment.

Truk, as the main island in the district was called then (it has since been renamed Chook, which more closely corresponds to the way the name is pronounced there), is a spectacularly beautiful island, a fantasy of sloping green mountainsides rising from translucent water, palm trees leaning from the shore, thickly foliated jungle so steep and dense that almost all the population is concentrated on the thin strip of lowland near the water's edge. Occupied and colonized by the Japanese in the early part of the last century, it was the site of some military action during the Second World War, a kind of reverse Pearl Harbor in fact. You can still see the masts of sunken Japanese war boats in the harbor, and, in spite of its great distance from population centers (1,000 miles east of the Philippines and north of New Guinea; 3,000 miles southwest of Hawaii), the island has become a magnet for scuba divers from all parts of the globe: they drop down onto the decks of those ships, squeeze through doorways, ogle the officers' mess with its table settings still intact.

There was a one-runway airport and a small ragged strip of stores at the northern end of the island of Truk, but the Peace Corps moved us south and west, to the more primitive section, a hamlet called Sapuk. In Sapuk we stayed with Trukese families and attended classes six days a week at the Catholic high school on the hill. It was the immersion method of language training, and it worked. I lived in a home with twenty-two Trukese people ranging in age from a year to sixty years, only one of whom had any understanding of English. There was a smelly outhouse at the edge of the trees out back, and, near the front door, a rain barrel that collected water from the roof. No electricity, no TV, no radio, no car, no air-conditioning or heating, no carpets or chairs or beds.

At night, when the brief, wild, tropical downpours passed through Sapuk, hundreds of the thumb-sized beetles we called "Guam Eagles" would crawl in under the eaves for safety, marching right up the rafters that supported the ceiling of my little sleeping room. They would crowd and bump like ticket holders pushing through a gate at Fenway Park, their hard exoskeletons knocking against the tin roof with an eerie ticking that could be heard clearly whenever the drumming of the rain eased for a moment. Without fail, two or three of them would lose their grip and fall onto the floor. I would be lying there on my woven pandanus mat, in pitch blackness. The unfortunate ones could not seem to open their wings fast enough—perhaps because they were falling upside down —and they struck the floor with an audible *click*, paused for a few seconds to get over the shock, righted themselves, then crawled in a determined way toward the nearest source of heat, which happened to be me. There are not many feelings that can compare to lying on the floor in a foreign place, in the dark, mostly naked, and feeling a two-inch-long beetle attach itself fiercely to the soft flesh at the inside of your thigh.

Despite the burning equatorial sun, the ubiquitous insects and stomach troubles, I was happy in Sapuk. The members of my extended host family—headed by a man named Samurai and a woman named Miako, and graced with two lovely young daughters named Xenifia and Nanci—were exceptionally kind and generous to me, washing my clothes, cooking my meals, building me a private bathing stall from saplings and sheets of plastic. In the morning there would be a breakfast of salted fish and rice, or octopus and tapioca, then I'd make the long walk up to Xavier High School and sit in classrooms all day with the other Peace Corps trainees, repeating phrases like: *Kop wene feine ia?* Where are you going? and *Met ka fuuri ikenai?* What are you doing today? and discovering that concepts I'd assumed to be basic to humanity had not been part of Trukese society until the white or yellow men arrived. There were, for instance, no words for "late" or "early" in Trukese: if you arrived late, you'd simply "come slow;" early and you'd "come fast." With the exception of the word *marram'*, which meant both "moon" and "month," and *rahn*, which meant "day," all the time expressions were English cognates: *minich, awa, wik, ier.* Left to their own devices, the islanders had never invented a word for "enough," and now used the bastardization nuf, as if the whole notion of insufficiency had been imported. "Toilet" and "movie" – *penjo* and *kachito*—had been borrowed from the Japanese, *Got* (as one being rather than a cluster of spirits) from the German. And dogs—raised on the islands as a food crop—were called *comeah*, which is what the islanders heard when English or American visitors tried, always in vain, to convince a mongrel to venture close and be petted.

After classes ended for the day, there were other things to learn—how to behave in tropical waters, for instance. I spent a lot of time snorkeling off the stone dock near Samurai and Miako's house, working my way out to the coral reef offshore and losing myself in schools of surgeonfish and angelfish, improbably beautiful kaleidoscopes of swirling, darting color. The abundance of fish attracted an abundance of sharks, but they were black-tipped reef sharks for the most part and not especially interested in human flesh. During training we'd learned that the safest way of dealing with them was to float motionless until they'd finished their curious sniffing and probing of the reef, and swum away. In the hundred yards of clear water between shore and the band of coral reef there were stingrays and barracuda, groupers twice my weight, eels, stone-fish, sea urchins, needlefish, turtles, clams, snails, lobster, angelfish, flying fish, lionfish with their venomous quills, coral knobs of various shapes, sizes, and colors, grasses, waving reeds—after Truk, even the best aquariums have never been able to amaze me.

With the help of Samurai and his son-in-law Antonio, I began to learn the art of spearfishing. Micronesians propel the spear not with a gun but with a loop of surgical tubing used more or less like a slingshot. Upon being impaled on the six-foot spear, a fish flaps and struggles, flailing about, sinking slowly to the sandy bottom. It's exactly the kind of motion that attracts sharks, and so, once I finally managed to spear a fish, I learned to kill it quickly, island-style, by placing its head between my back teeth and biting down hard. Nothing was killed for sport on those islands; everything we speared ended up on the table— fried in oil, smoked, or salted, served with breadfruit, taro, papaya, coconut, white rice, bananas, tapioca, and often as not covered with flies.

I loved to spearfish—the challenge of it, the beauty of the undersea world, even the danger—and I loved the diet, too. What I didn't love, what rasped against my pride like a handsaw blade against flesh, was feeling uncoordinated and inept so much of the time. I couldn't climb the thin palm trunks with a three-foot machete in one hand the way even young island boys did. I was a clumsy swimmer and spearfisherman, a twenty-five-year-old with a baby's vocabulary, pathetically vulnerable to the sun, unable to see in the dark, unsure of island etiquette.

Worst of all, I was not being of help to anyone, though I told myself all that would change once I shipped out to the atoll and began the real work I'd been sent there to do. The job description that had enticed me to volunteer for a Micronesian assignment was two pages long and full of important-sounding duties. I was to be a Municipal Development Advisor, living out on one of Truk's far-flung outer islands, collecting the laws the Trukese had lived by for hundreds of years, organizing them into a charter. When all the islands were chartered, the district of Truk would be able to free itself of the yoke of United Nations trusteeship and establish itself as an independent state.

In late September I expressed my gratitude to the host family with gifts of rice, oranges, and jackknives, and caught the field-trip ship out to the Hall Islands, a full day's sail to the north. Probably until my last breath I will remember the feeling of climbing down from that ship into a small skiff and riding toward the island of Murilo. Named after the sixteenth-century Spanish painter (though spelled with one less "I"), it was a tiny place, no more than fifty acres in all, with a sandy summit that stood six feet above sea level. Palm fronds glinting in the sunlight, a few dozen houses with corrugated iron roofs, swarms of children running naked near the water's edge – Murilo was surrounded by vast stretches of sea and sky. I had never been in country where the mark made by humanity was so inconsequential, the presence of nature so immense and pure, so overwhelming. For a moment, before we drew close enough to hear the voices of people on shore, I felt face to face with an enormous and mysterious presence, beside which all the commotion and achievement of humankind was positively Lilliputian. The feeling lasted only a few breaths, then the skiff made its way through the small surf and ground up on a beach, and I was caught again in the web of human manners and mores.

For a while I was happy on Murilo, too. A man named Johales and his wife, Aruko, took over for Samurai and Miako, cooking, washing, and coming into my hut at night with their children to entertain me with stories and a cappella songs. From the time I'd had my worldview turned inside out, somewhere in the middle of Siberia, I had been looking for a life like this: a life unfettered by politics, technology, and money. I wanted to go back and back, deep into the formation of human society, and find what was bare and true. Murilo was as close as I could ever hope to come to that untainted vision, as "pure" as anyplace on earth. There was no need for cash on the island, no electricity, no plumbing, no police. I slept on a straw mat on the floor of a small concrete box of a house, used the jungle as my toilet, washed myself with brackish water from one of the mid-island wells, ate, for the most part, only what was caught in the ocean and harvested from the trees. Once a week I sat in a tiny room at the back of the makeshift schoolhouse and talked to the Peace Corps Office in Truk on a scratchy shortwave radio while students chanted the multiplication tables at top volume a few feet away. Other than that I did not speak English, or have contact with Americans, or leave the atoll. The field-trip ship was not scheduled to return for three months.

The only real problem, beside the awful heat and the various infections—ear, urinary tract, intestinal—I'd brought with me from Truk, was that there was absolutely nothing to do. On the day after I arrived I'd stood before the council of men that gathered every Tuesday, and said I'd come to assist them in the writing of a charter, and that I would offer English lessons, too, if anyone wanted them. After that meeting, the island chief, a three-hundred pound neighbor of mine named Marcus, came up and thanked me, welcomed me, said he'd let me know when he was ready to start the charter project.

A week went by, and though I saw Marcus almost every day on the sandy paths near my house, he did not mention the charter. Two weeks went by. No one wanted English lessons. My stomach troubles worsened to the point where I had to eat almost continuously in order to avoid feeling nauseous had to make frequent trips into the trees behind my house with a roll of toilet paper in my pocket. I consoled myself by taking walks along the island's sandy circumference, facing down the snarling dogs there, spearing fish in the tepid lagoon. Every morning after breakfast I waded in with my snorkel and spear, reappearing two hours later with a string of three or four eight-inch fish dangling from a length of wire around my belt. Murilo's children, a raucous, happy bunch, would wait on the beach and follow me back to my house, laughing and shrieking and pointing at my puny catch. Their fathers, even their older brothers, would go out for a few minutes and return with half-a-dozen fish two feet long. But I could not dive as deep, or stay submerged as long, or shoot as accurately, and the penalty for that inexperience was this little parade of humiliation—a white Pied Piper striding along in the blazing midday sun with a string of naked brown kids behind him, laughing so hard they sometimes toppled over in the hot dust with their feet kicking up in the air and tears squirting out the sides of their eyes.

Slowly, hot empty afternoon by hot empty afternoon, my mood began to sour. I begged Johales and the other men to let me work with them, cutting the white meat out of coconut shells, or paddling off in the outrigger canoes to hunt turtle eggs. But, with typical Micronesian indirectness, they resisted: glancing away, changing the subject, saying yes and then never coming by my house at the appointed hour. "We don't want you to get hurt," Johales said when I pressed him. "There's no hospital here, no doctor. If you hurt, yourself cutting copra it would be a disgrace for this island, for the Chief, for all of us." I told him I wasn't worried about being hurt, I wasn't even worried about dying. What I was worried about was going crazy from idleness. But he only nodded, averted his eyes, said he would see me at dinner, and that, in the meantime, I should rest.

Rest was at the bottom of the list of things I wanted. When I tried to start work on the island legal system, I found out that one of the laws I was there to record prohibited any such project from beginning without permission from the chief. You could not request that permission; he had to volunteer it. Technically, I was not even allowed to have a conversation about the charter with a neighbor in the privacy of my own hut—though one friend named Luther sometimes broke that rule. When I began to feel that the weeks of boredom would crush the life out of me, I decided to ignore island etiquette: I approached Marcus and asked him bluntly if I could begin. He put a hand on my shoulder and said, *"Ewer, Rolan, ewer"* Sure, Roland, sure. I'll let you know when.

More spearfishing, more midnight diarrhea dashes out into the trees behind my house, more hot afternoons spent making fifteen-minute circumambulations and sitting in the broiling shade fanning flies off my chest and legs. There were no single females over the age of eight on Murilo; during the day there was no comfortable place to sit and read or write—the house too hot, the outdoor shade too buggy; there was no possibility of solitude, staple of my psychological diet. My closest friend was a rat who visited in the middle of the night, knocking bottles of vitamins off my knee-high table and rooting around in my stash of ship biscuits and toilet paper. I chased him one night, knocked him out cold with my spear, but didn't have the heart to kill him.

The weekly radio-net was some comfort, but in the fourth week the radio lost its charge . . . just as the medical officer was telling me—over the gleeful shouts of two-time-two-equals-four in the next room—that they'd found some kind of worms in the stool sample I'd left at the Truk Hospital. In a desperate attempt to escape the boredom and to prove myself useful and manly, I went spear-fishing in the huge surf off the back beach and came within a whisker of drowning. I started to carve a chess set with my Swiss Army knife, taped a message for Amanda which, when I listen to it now, sounds like the rantings of a stranded sailor.

After I'd been on Murilo a month or so, a Japanese lobster ship stopped at the island, bringing with it medicine to kill my worms and a package from Amanda that included candy, a music tape, and a lock of her chestnut-colored hair. I dreamt about her at night, squirming on my woven mat.

At last, after I'd been on Murilo four-and-a-half weeks, Marcus ordered the men to assemble and we had our first meeting on the charter project. It was like a dose of morphine. The men (in most other ways given the full measure of respect on the island, women were not allowed to participate in its governance) were incredibly astute about the importance of a precise code of laws, amazingly forward-looking in their questions and caveats, far more interested in the making of their own democracy than Americans have been for the last couple hundred years. I fairly floated out of the room that day. At last, I was of some use in the world. At last I was helping.

I made my report to Marcus—who had not attended—and he nodded thoughtfully, patted my shoulder, and told me he'd let me know when I could schedule another meeting. Weeks went by and I did not hear from him. It occurred to me that the kind of democracy I'd come to the island to promote was going to put Marcus out of a job. He'd been royalty since birth, and now, once my project was completed, the charters collected, and the islands granted some form of democratic status, he would be just another fat guy pooping in the palms.

Befuddled as I was by rampant hormones, vicious sun headaches, infected scratches, infected ears, an infected urinary tract, the side effects of the antiworm medicine, and the incredible force of the equatorial heat, it nevertheless began to be clear to me that I wasn't doing the slightest good for anyone there on Murilo. I was wasting my life, my youth, turning sickly and lazy and dull. Once, a young man cut his thigh to the bone with a machete and I helped carry him into one of the houses, told the woman treating him that if she didn't remove the tourniquet, he'd lose his leg and perhaps his life, assisted her as she cleaned and sewed up the wound. Once, I gave two aspirin to a friend with an abscessed tooth. Once, I fished a drowned rat out of the cistern, with my macho Micronesian friends gagging and groaning all around, and threw it into the sea. But set against the growing momentum of my feelings of uselessness, those contributions seemed utterly without merit.

Even more disheartening was the fact that my simple notions about rich and poor had been made muddy and vague. This was no small matter. I had built a huge, fancy ship out of my idealistic philosophies, my goodness, myself-sacrifice . . . and sailed it right into a moral swamp. With their plywood huts and bare feet, the Micronesians matched my image of Third World poverty well enough. But the fact was that, on balance, they were better off than the Americans I knew. They did not work for money, but to feed their families, and they spent long hours just hanging out—talking, playing cards, sometimes lying in the shallows with all but their stomachs, mouths, and noses submerged. With a few exceptions, the marriages seemed like happy ones; certainly the children were happy. The Murilans lived in near-perfect harmony with nature, had an inherent spirituality, an utter lack of stress, of greed, of envy. They suckled each other's children, shared catches of fish, passed cigarettes around the circle at night so that everyone got equal puffing time. I'd stumbled upon a kind of perfect socialist non-state, and was messing with it. During training on Guam I'd asked a veteran volunteer what she thought of her work in the islands, and without missing a beat she answered: "*They* should be sending Peace Corps volunteers to *us*."

It was true that the men and women were old by the time they reached their sixties, but they seemed unafraid of death, often making jokes about it. Of course they wanted to live longer, healthier lives. ("Rolan'," one neighbor asked me after working up to it for some time, "is it normal for people to shit blood?") Of course they would have welcomed indoor plumbing if it meant not having to lug buckets of water from the well. Of course they would have wanted the kind of medical care that would make giving birth safer, and the infant mortality rate lower (as it was, many island women had started to travel to the hospital on Truk to have their babies). But, with the kind of wisdom and prescience I'd seen in the one charter meeting, at least some of them understood that there was a price to be paid for those luxuries and comforts, that their lives would be changed irrevocably, that, even without Walkmans and microwaves, they had a good thing going here, on their spot of sand in the middle of the ocean, a place where there hadn't been so much as a fistfight in ten years.

I didn't have a good thing going there, though. Hour by hour, my various illnesses and the moral ambiguity of my situation sawed away at the edifice of my spiritual pride and physical toughness. I thought, bitterly, of the glowing, two-page job description. Municipal Development Advisor, my ass. I thought of words from a letter my aunt had sent when I was in training: "If you're unhappy there, come home." I thought of Amanda, the pleasures of sex, work, ice cubes in cold glasses of coffee. Sitting on the dead coral of the back beach, staring out over the rough, hot sea, it began to seem to me that I had spent my life chained in place by the praise of family and friends, an obedient son, a dutiful Catholic, a good student and employee. Sex, swearing, drinking, drugs—I had started all those things at a later age than almost everyone I knew, and even then made only tentative forays into the exhilarating territory of the forbidden. What would it be like to really fail at something for a change? To splash myself with the bright paint of disgrace? What if I told the Peace Corps to go to hell, and just went home?

In the interior realm, at least, not many things are more painful than a battle with one's own pride. Decorating the image we make of ourselves, there, are always certain salient positives—the belief that we are intelligent or unselfish, likable, capable, graceful, strong—and when one or two of those proud vessels break against the shoals and begin to sink, a particular kind of panic can set in. The drowning demon of pride clutches at anything to save itself—it blames, rationalizes, lashes out.

In my case, there was an easy target. The Peace Corps had advertised itself as "the toughest job you'll ever love," set itself up as an alternative to the bourgeois life of Middle America. I fancied myself as above that life, better than the police lieutenant with his backyard pool and litany of complaint. But there had turned out to be no job, little to love, nothing in me that was as strong, or as good, or as selfless, as the scenes from my inflated self-image promised.

In November, when the field-trip ship anchored off Murilo, I packed my bags and climbed aboard. Johales and Aruko were hurt, I knew that. And Marcus would suffer from a mild case of embarrassment in front of his fellow chiefs. But I was as petulant and pissed-off as a spurned lover. My great gesture of help had sputtered and spit, my grandiose notions had been reduced to sweat and mosquito bites. My proud stoicism—honed by years of hard exercise in crew shells, the discomforts of life in the Soviet Union, and six ascetic months in a cold house in Vermont—had been crushed to bits in the Central Pacific. It wasn't the heat that had beaten me. It wasn't the constant illness. It wasn't even the lack of a woman. What had cut my willpower off at the knees was the hot blade of my own angry pride: the world wasn't as simple as I'd supposed; the urge to do good is a nice idea—I believe in it to this day—but on Murilo I started to understand that, deep in the waters of individual psychology, it swims close alongside the shark of self-centeredness and ego. Try spearing and killing a shark like that; try even to be still, and let your own panic subside, and watch it attentively as it probes and sniffs, and eventually sidles away.

It was a thirty-hour flight from Truk back to the East Coast, with long delays in Honolulu and L.A. I did not call my parents until I landed in Newark, at six A.M. "Pa," I said, when my father picked up the phone. "I'm in New Jersey. I'm coming home."

And, without even the smallest hesitation, he said: "Good."

For years and years after I came back from Micronesia, just the sound of the words "Peace Corps" filled me with shame. It had been a dream of mine since high school, a program I believed in (and still believe in), and, despite my rationalizations on Murilo's back beach, I had failed at it, completely, resoundingly, irrevocably. Before I'd set off for the islands, my father and mother had organized a huge going-away party, invited the uncles, aunts, and cousins, all the neighbors, all of our friends. The guests had shaken my hand, hugged me, told me what a good person I was, what a good Christian, how courageous . . . And here I was, less than six months into my two-year contract, standing at the carousel at Logan Airport with my fishing spear in one hand, and all sorts of infections in my innards. My parents took me out for pancakes and milk, and I slept for sixteen hours straight, and woke up a failure.

I had been a conceited boy, proud of my brains and coordination, of my family, of my "goodness, in ways I couldn't begin to disguise. There had been some bad times, naturally—in sports, in my nascent romantic life, even in school—but I'd always cruised blithely through, coasting on the affection I'd been surrounded by as a child, assuming, as Joan Didion so perfectly put it, "that lights would always turn green for me."

Micronesia was the place where the first light went red. The light went red, the car slid off the road, rolled over, and I crawled out. Battered and broken, I stayed with my parents a week or two, then went to live with Amanda in Allston. From time to time now, twenty-two years later, some of the illnesses I first encountered in Micronesia rise up again to haunt me, cellular ghosts from the dark intestinal reaches, immortal. From time to time, an interior groan sounds from the old psychological scars—the way a bad weld on a bridge will moan and creak when the load of traffic is too great. Every few months I'll have a phone conversation with a friend in California who went into the Peace Corps for reasons similar to mine, was assigned to Truk with me, volunteered for duty on an outer atoll not very different from Murilo, quit on the same day I did and rode the field-trip ship back to the main island, convincing himself with a string of logical arguments that it would have been foolish to stay. We still joke about the experience, pass back and forth a word or two of the beautiful language, but even now there is something in the background, a whispered *failure, failure, failure,* penance of proud men. A little sting of shame circles the edges of the conversation, like a lonely white man walking desolate along an atoll's sandy rim in the middle of a hot, empty day.

Low-Rent Rendezvous

Amanda and I lived, together with a friend of hers, in a two-bedroom flat in a sagging apartment house in the Allston section of Boston. We were living in sin, as people used to say (just the two of us; Amanda's friend was sinless). That is, we had immersed ourselves in the passionate feast of young adulthood without sanction of the Church, the State, or our elders, and without pinning our futures together with any kind of eternal, breakable promise. Our choice of each other had more to do with endocrinology than with logic; our choice of Allston more to do with chance, or fate, than with any carefully thought-out plan about what we wanted from our lives. But plan or not, societal sanction or not, lust or love or karma, we had, on short notice, made the decision to mix the volatile chemicals of two very different histories. We would share a bedroom, in Allston, in the apartment Amanda already shared with a friend named Charlotte. We would see where that might lead us.

Allston, in those days, was a lower-middle-class jambalaya of students, musicians, recent immigrants, and working families whose people had lived there, on the western edge of downtown, since the end of the previous century. On warm nights, saxophone scales and Red Sox play-by-play floated out through apartment windows, and guitarists and drummers sat on wooden front steps, improvising for small audiences. The sidewalks and gutters were decorated with weeds, paper litter, bottle caps and bottles, black blots of old chewing gum, butts of cigarettes, Popsicle sticks and pop-tops, the occasional condom. Empty parking spaces were rare as winning scratch tickets. And the cars that lined the curbs were spotted with rust, ticketed, dented, duly registered and probably insured, and marking quite precisely their owners' station in the wider world.

Our apartment occupied the front right quarter of the second floor of a house on Linden Street—I will call it 926 Linden, but there is no such number. It consisted of a windowless bathroom, a counterless kitchen that two people could not walk through at the same time, and two bedrooms separated by a parlor, on one side of which stood a fireplace that could not be used, and on the other a bay window looking down on the street. Our roommate, Charlotte, was employed in Harvard Square at a place called Belgian Fudge. In the evenings she would bring home small white cardboard boxes filled with the unsold chunks and leavings—lumps of penuche, slivers of chocolate, maple-walnut crumbs—a mix of shapes, colors, and tastes as diverse and curious as the neighborhood's.

During that fall and the unusually cold winter that followed it, our street, 926 Linden especially, took on the aspect of a dreary carnival: pockets of mirth and absurdity against a background of want and petty meanness. The list of sideshow acts was headed, as any self-respecting apartment-house carnival should be, by a miserly landlord. After weeks of deflecting requests to fix the drooping bathroom sink, he came by one afternoon when all three of us were at work, let himself in, and made the repair by propping a length of two-by-four under the sink's front lip. This might have been acceptable if he hadn't sawed off the two-by-four an inch too short, and decided to make up the difference by taking a bar of soap—our soap—and jamming it in between wood and porcelain.

He is to be forgiven for that, I suppose, and for taking his telephone off the hook when the furnace ran out of oil on a freezing holiday weekend in February, and for insisting on playing the role of decent and beleaguered small businessman, oppressed on one side by the priggish safety regulations of the Commonwealth of Massachusetts, and on the other by a menagerie of self-centered tenants. It must not have been easy, presiding over the 926 Linden Street show.

Across the hall from us lived a high-school science teacher who moonlighted as a marijuana salesman; downstairs, a deranged teenaged brother and sister, just blossoming into juvenile delinquency, who liked to amuse themselves by throwing borrowed shopping carts down the back steps twenty or thirty times at a go; and, in the apartment directly behind ours, a tough, thirtyish, artificially blond divorcee named Patricia, who had a boyfriend

115

we sometimes heard, late at night, but never saw.

Two pieces of sheetrock and some air separated Patricia's domestic predicament from our own, and since the apartments abutted each other at the bedrooms, she and her lover sometimes disturbed our sleep with their late-night antics. It wasn't their lovemaking that woke us—if they made love in that room they did so quietly—but their fights. Actually, even their fights were quiet ones until the last few exchanges. In the later rounds we would hear voices rising through the wall as if someone on the other side were tapping the volume button on a remote at five-second intervals. It was the anger station they were playing in there. But if you listened beyond the anger you could trace a clear route backward in time to the hurt station, the fear of failing again station, the not enough money station. After a few minutes of increasingly nasty exchanges, Patricia would invariably introduce the term "fucking prick"—sign that the end was near—and not very long after that we would hear the door slam and the boyfriend stomp out. I still remember the sound of his boots on the creaking pine floor of our hallway.

For reasons we could not ascertain, something to do with biorhythms, no doubt, these arguments always occurred between one-thirty and three o'clock in the morning. Amanda worked the lunch and dinner shifts at a nice French restaurant, and would be awakened in her first hour or two of sleep. And I'd found a position as a taxi driver, early shift, and had to be up before dawn. To make matters worse, immediately following her lover's loud departure Patricia would soothe herself by playing music at top volume. The music was always the same—the Amazing Rhythm Aces' pop-country classic: "Third Rate Romance, Low-Rent Rendezvous." Amanda and I came to know the chorus by heart:

You don't look like my type
But I guess you'll do
Third-rate romance
Low-rent rendezvous

I've never done this kinda thing before
Have you?
Third-rate romance
Low-rent raw-awn dey vou

We pounded on the wall with the heels of our hands. When that didn't work, I climbed out of bed, went into the cold hallway in boxer shorts and a T-shirt and banged on Patricia's door until she yelled, "Okay, alright," through the wood panels and turned off the record player. And on nights when neither of those relatively polite approaches silenced the musical echo of our neighbor's grief, we called the police, who responded a couple of times—more boots in the hallway—then, sensibly enough, stopped responding.

All of us had work schedules that kept us out of the house for long hours, and so, in the early going, neither Amanda nor Charlotte nor I ever bumped into Patricia in the hallway or on the walk leading up to our tilted front porch. We knew her name from the mailbox in the entranceway, from her boyfriend's exasperated shouts. Based on the early-morning arguments, Amanda and I imagined we'd formed a kind of intimacy with Patricia: her voice, her frustrations, a piece of her life regularly found its way into our bedroom. But, during that fall and winter, I do not ever remember catching more than a glimpse of her. I remember conversations about her, but never with her, unless brief, heated exchanges through a locked door count as conversation. It was as if she were a creature from another dimension, an irritating dream-presence, a phantom.

Despite the thumps on her wall, Patricia must have imagined us, too, as not quite real. She never came over in the mornings and apologized, the way an ordinary neighbor might. She never thought to leave us a note—angry, contrite, or otherwise. After we realized that even the police couldn't help us, we learned to just bang on the wall a few times and roll over, to accept the bedroom wars as we accepted Allston's dearth of parking spaces, and 926 Linden's periodic lack of heat. The fights went on and on— not every night, but regularly Amanda endured this state of things without complaining to the landlord (who, to be fair, had rented the apartment to two tenants and it now housed three at the same rate). And I continued to get out of bed at quarter to four in the morning and ferry people about the streets of Boston in my yellow cab on a few hours of broken-up sleep.

Though it provided an income of about two dollars an hour, I had a real affection for driving cab. On days when the fighting next door hadn't broken up our sleep, I loved waking up early in the cool apartment, washing quietly at the propped-up sink, then taking breakfast standing in our three-foot by ten-foot kitchen with the house and the neighborhood still buried in the knock and hum of the city night.

Having so recently returned from Micronesia, from all those mornings of feeling useless and bored, it meant something to me to be able to dial the taxi company and say: "926 Linden Street, Allston, for a driver coming in." Buoyed by that thin sense of fraternity, I would walk out into the corridor and down the stairs with a notebook under one arm, and stand in the unheated foyer until the roof lights of a Checker cab came into view.

I loved that moment: going out the front door and down our walk in the cold air, in a whirl of fat snowflakes, or a stiff January breeze off the Charles. I liked making ten minutes of small talk with the driver—how his night had been, which neighborhoods he usually worked. We made the traffic-less trip down Commonwealth Avenue, past blinking yellow lights and idling police cars, then turned onto St. Botolph Street, where the same toothless street-walker waited on the corner hoping for one last client, and the Company garage loomed, plain-faced and tattered, so much life inside.

After filling out the lease forms with Abe, the night clerk, who chewed on an unlit stogie and kept a crowbar against his stool, like a cane, for protection (it was a rough neighborhood, and the office business was conducted-exclusively in cash), I'd walk down the ramp to the basement level, where the concrete ceiling was stained and dripping, and yellow taxis stood close together in double rows. A black teenaged boy worked there, washing cabs and moving them into place for the day shift drivers. Wet jeans, soaked sneakers, straight spine, he moved about in his damp fluorescent world with a dignity that sang its chorus in my own heart. We were the world's menial laborers, he and I and Amanda, underappreciated, invisible, carrying beneath our plain exteriors great universes of dream. I'd exchange a few words with him, tip him with a folded-up dollar when he brought the cab around, then drive up the ramp and out into the city, floating along in my creaking yellow vessel, filled with an odd, drowsy satisfaction.

Prostitutes, airline crews, and the occasional all-night reveler made up the clientele of the early morning. There were not many drivers on the job then, and we moved around the city in our dark orbits, watching for each other like insects whose rhythms bring them out to mate only at certain times, flashing a greeting with our headlights, clinging week after week to the same pockets of safety and warmth.

But the first hour was a quiet one, a time of muted echoes in the avenues, of urban contemplation. Without yet having earned anything, I'd spend another dollar on a cup of coffee and a cruller at the Dunkin' Donuts on Boylston Street, then stand the cab in front of the Lenox Hotel. There, slouched behind the wheel with the engine running and the heater on, I'd tinker with the outline of a book I was dreaming about writing, looking up from time to time to study the sky between the buildings as it moved from indigo through the most delicate pastel shades of winter pink and blue.

After a little while—five minutes, twenty-five minutes—out from the Lenox lobby would step a businessman or a pilot in need of a lift to Logan. I'd set his bags in the trunk, take my place on the scarred leatherette seat, turn on the meter, pull the shift into Drive, glide along the shadowy streets and through the tunnel that runs under Boston Harbor, and deliver him to the terminal like a seasoned professional. The eleven hours that followed would be a tapestry of similar expeditions: voyages from one corner of the city to another, traffic lights, sirens, the comfort of a ticking meter; long waits in the airport taxi pool or at reserved sections of curb with the Company radio scratching and squawking and all the busyness of Boston, of life, passing in parade beyond the windows.

Though I was a city kid by birth, as far as the art of driving a taxi was concerned I might as well have been a farm-boy from Saskatchewan with a learner's permit in his wallet. Instead of cruising the labyrinthine alleys of the financial district, where executives stood on every corner with a flight to catch and a raised arm, I kept to the more easily navigated residential streets of the Back Bay, content to sit for thirty minutes between fares and catch up on what I considered my real work, reading and writing. Instead of driving Monday through Friday, which would have made me a full-time employee and entitled me to split the meter charges with the Company, fifty-fifty, and keep all the tips, I drove only three days a week, and leased the cab—which meant that, out of a sixty-five-dollar average daily gross, I ended up netting about twenty-five.

When the weather was good, and when I wanted a break from reading, I'd get out of the cab and sip coffee with the older drivers waiting in front of the Hilton or Ritz-Carlton. Shortcuts, one-way traps, best and worst places to look for fares at different times of day, tricks for staying out of trouble—the lore of the profession was handed down to me in short blooms of conversation all over the city. "First rule to remember," one veteran driver said as we caught a breath of air near Boston Common, "never, ever, get out of the cab in an altercation, alright?" I kept to that commandment, at first, and didn't have much trouble. A few arguments with cranky or drug-addled customers; the mild abuse of one delivery truck driver who yelled "Fucking nickel-chaser!" out his side window because he thought I had tooted the horn at him the instant a traffic light went green. (It was the driver behind me.)

Cabdriving introduced me to neck pain and hemorrhoids, the days were peppered with small aggravations and petty conflicts, but even through the haze that formed after hours behind the wheel, I enjoyed the work. There was a certain pleasure to be taken from listening to the dispatcher's sing-song patter ("One-fifty Tremont. One-fifty Tremont. Who's near Tremont? Charles? Boylston? Beacon Hill? Let's go ladies and gentlemen. Who can take a regular from One-fifty Tremont to Brookline?") and a certain satisfaction in feeling part of the army of nickel-chasers prowling the metropolis in every kind of weather, having conversations with judges and psychologists, strippers and drunks. There was a sense of collegiality among the Checker drivers, a frosting of danger to the mundanities of the twelve-hour day, a short list of secret codes we were required to memorize in order to protect each other and ourselves. And, every now and then, there was the opportunity to do a good deed: carry an octogenarian's grocery bags up to a third-floor apartment, or pluck a prostitute off a corner at five A.M. and take her out of a neighborhood where locked cab doors and a two-way radio counted for something.

Once, sitting in a long string of cabs at a luxury hotel that stands on the border between one of Boston's richest and one of its poorest neighborhoods, I watched an African American brother and sister—they must have been ten and twelve years old—make their way down the line of taxis idling in front of me. Technically, it was against the law to refuse a fare based on destination. But, like most other American cities, Boston has sections where black cab drivers do not like to work, and sections where white cab drivers do not like to work, and certain streets, housing projects, and neighborhoods where no one likes to work. And so, in practice, it wasn't uncommon for cabbies to refuse to venture into places with a reputation for trouble. And so I was disturbed, but not surprised, when it became clear to me that the brother and sister were asking one white driver after the next to take them home, and one white driver after the next was turning his back.

When the pair approached me, after eight refusals, it

turned out that there was another wrinkle to the story: they said they had no money on them but would get some at home, if I took them there. They told me where home was—an infamous neighborhood—and I let them into the cab, drove to the address, and waited nervously while they disappeared into one of the dilapidated houses on a street that seemed to have no connection whatsoever to the neat, safe world we'd just left. After a little while I tooted the horn, and after another minute or so the girl reappeared with a handful of crumpled bills and some change. I drove back toward the safety of downtown feeling proud of that small errand, in a time when there was not very much else in my life to feel proud about.

Though a driver from our company had been robbed and shot to death, in his cab a few days before I started work, I kept to the practice of never refusing a fare. Three-quarters of my driving was done during the daylight hours, and nine-tenths of it in safe neighborhoods, so this was not an especially courageous decision, but I held it up in my mind's eye like a secret trophy. I had less than a hundred dollars in the bank, no health insurance to set against the various illnesses I'd carried home from the islands, no warm winter coat, no inheritance to look forward to, no mutual funds, no 401(K), no practical life-plan, nothing to show for my fancy education and world travel besides a hundred pages of ballpoint scribbling and half a share of a bed in a drafty apartment.

To make matters worse, the first blush of our infatuation was already fading. Amanda and I did not wake anyone in the middle of the night with our troubles, but we knew some troubles then—jealousies, different expectations and tastes, family backgrounds that seemed, on some days, absolutely irreconcilable. She saved, I spent. She held her feelings in, I poured them out. She liked a sense of community, I wanted solitude. We fought, sulked, made up with a great sense of relief, enjoyed a stretch of harmony, fought again. There were weeks at a time when all the promise of my college years, and all my bright hopes of finding a true love seemed to have been reduced to ashes, leaving me clinging to imaginary heroisms in my rattling taxi, struggling to keep my head just above the turbulent waters in which some of my clients, and most of our neighbors, seemed to have long ago drowned.

Once, on a dreary February day when I arrived late at the garage and had to settle for one of the older and less dependable cabs, I was sitting in line at Massachusetts General Hospital when the floor just to the left of the brake pedal burst into flames. A wiser person might have taken this as some kind of omen, a hint from the gods that a career change was in order. But I stamped out the blaze with my workboot, drove back to the garage, signed out a more wholesome set of wheels, and went stubbornly about what I took to be my business.

Once or twice I was "beaten" for the fare, as we used to say—the customer jumped out and ran instead of paying. Once, a threesome of young North Enders who were setting off on vacation tipped me ten dollars on top of their ten-dollar airport fare. Once, another driver was being threatened by a back-seat psychopath, and yelled out the secret code over the radio, and within a minute eleven cabs were surrounding him in front of the Boston Public Library, flashers blinking, drivers strutting about like a UN peacekeeping posse with beards and bellies: Ukrainians, Ethiopians, Irishmen, Poles, native-born Americans with inkstains on their fingers.

But most days were uneventful. Airport runs and nurses going home; rain, sleet, Boston's felonious drivers and tepid winter sun.

Ironically enough, the only place I ever had any real trouble was in the North End, the Italian section of the city, where, seventy years earlier, my father's parents had lived in the first blush of their own state- and church-sanctioned cohabitation. On that day I had been driving for seven hours on a poor night's sleep and a breakfast of Belgian fudge and coffee. The dispatcher called out over the radio that a cab was needed on Hanover Street and gave the number of the house. I sped off in that direction, and had almost reached the address when one of the neighborhood teenagers took it upon himself to cross very slowly in front of the cab and berate me with some rough language for not being careful enough on his turf. Not in a mood to just let him have his say, I put the shift in Park, got out of the cab, shouted back. A small crowd gathered. After a few exchanges that escalated at roughly the same rate as the fights between Patricia and her boyfriend, the teenager surprised me with a fairly competent left hook, which I fairly competently blocked. In the next instant, a friend of his standing behind me reached around and drove his fist into the socket of my left eye.

Someone from the block—a two-hundred-pound someone—had the grace to step into that little circle of trouble with me, push the assailants away, maneuver me back against the side of the cab, and suggest that I leave. I left. But before I left, in an attempt to rescue one little scrap of vanity from the afternoon, I rolled down the window and said: "Everybody's tough in his own neighborhood"—the best line I could think of on short notice. I called in a warning to the other Checker drivers who might wander up that street in my wake, then, half-blind, drove to the nearest hospital, where a kind intern checked out the eye without charging me.

Amanda was, away that night, visiting family. I have a memory of myself, lying in the bed at 926 Linden Street, cold, tired, with a sore face and fifty dollars to my name. "What am I doing?" I muttered into the darkness. "What am I doing? What am I doing with my life?" The answer, I suppose, though I would not have been able to offer it to myself in quite such clear terms then, was that I was trying to live the artist's life.

The artist's life. True to my blurry image of it, an image made up of, one part creative rebellion, one part poverty, and one part honest labor, I drove cab only on Mondays, Wednesdays, and Saturdays. On the other days I'd grab the ninety-nine-cent breakfast special at a Greek coffee-shop on Harvard Avenue and walk to the Allston, Public Library, where I sat with ballpoint pen and legal pad for hours and hours and handwrote hundreds of pages about an arid little island in the Central Pacific. Eventually, with the help of several supportive friends and one true mentor, those scribblings would evolve into a novel. And eventually, twelve years later, that novel would be put into print by the Boston publishing house I used to drive my taxi past and wrap dreams around.

But I had no way of knowing that then. I wrote because, in certain moments, the world seemed vivid and splendid to me, a creature to be praised. And because I dreamed of finding a way of life that offered a freedom like the freedom offered by taxi-driving, only with a higher salary and a greater sense of creativity.

Amanda was flying a similar route away from the comfort of a regular paycheck, and our preference for adventure over security was a key ingredient in the glue that held us together then. (And now, after twenty years of marriage.)

After college, she had traveled alone through Mexico and Guatemala, then come to Boston and moved in with Charlotte on the strength of a single conversation. She had turned down a teaching position, most likely of lifetime tenure, at the prestigious Emma Willard School in Troy, New York. Though her parents' immigrant roots were three hundred years in the past, they were bound by the same sets of assumptions and values that bound my parents, a tight, neat worldview that Amanda wanted to stretch and mold a bit before climbing into.

She walked home late from the French restaurant in Coolidge Corner with a pocket full of tips and, on nights when I knew I could sleep past four A.M., I waited up for her with all the anticipation of a young lover. During our free hours, we ran windsprints on the neighborhood streets, drove her fickle Dodge Colt out to Revere Beach every month on the night of the full moon and treated ourselves to Kelly's Famous Roast Beef Sandwiches, onion rings, and cartons of chocolate milk. We cooked simple meals, made out in restaurants, read pop psychology and contemporary fiction. One of us brought home a case of scabies—a sort of invisible louse passed from human to human by casual contact—and we scratched and writhed and sprayed the mattress for weeks until we discovered the name for our affliction, and its cure.

It could be argued that, somewhere in the depths of our young minds, we knew that the life we were leading then—such a ragged mix of pleasure and struggle—was only a rough preliminary to a softer, more secure fate. Both of us had Brown degrees, after all, and I suppose we were partly insulated from the difficulties of those days by the promise of prosperity that, true or false, always accompanies a good education.

At the time, though, we lacked the comfort of perspective. Our fights, our jealousies, our various insecurities were excruciatingly real. The physical troubles I'd brought home from paradise were real, as were the apartment's wild variations in temperature, and late-night noise. The vigor of a youthful body goes only so far toward softening the strain of twelve hours in traffic, or ten hours of shuttling between kitchen and dining room carrying other people's meals. Though now it has taken on the sheen of slightly amusing history, our time in Allston was as raw and real to us then as the rent payment: two hundred seventy dollars a month, split three ways.

Charlotte put up with us not doing our share of the cleaning, and keeping her from the bathroom (which could be reached only through our bedroom) morning and night with our great physical enthusiasm for each other. We put up with her peculiar culinary concoctions and offbeat friends. And we all learned to put up with the landlord, especially as the worst of the winter passed and the leaky windows and capricious furnace did not matter so much.

But, month after month, it was not so easy to put up with Patricia, with being awakened by her middle-of-the-night cursing, her boyfriend's boots, her third-rate romance pressing so intimately against our own low-rent rendezvous.

In late March, after months of patience and one night of almost no sleep, I walked to the Allston courthouse and filled out an order summoning Patricia into court to swear before a judge that she would cease and desist from making excessive noise. The next ten nights were peaceful. I assumed the court order had been sent out immediately, that our neighbor had gone before the judge, resolved to change her ways.

But on a grim afternoon when the snowbanks along Boston's streets were black with soot, and the twilight descending upon the city seemed to promise only four more months of cold, I took a bus home from the garage, as usual, climbed the stairs to the second floor, as always, and found Patricia waiting for me there in the corridor. She was wearing a peasant blouse and jeans, she was holding the court order in her hand, there was a stream of tears dribbling down one side of her face. "Why do you hate me?" she said.

I explained that it wasn't a question of hatred, but of sleep. Why did she think we'd been pounding on her walls all those nights, banging on her door? How did she think it felt to be awakened by people screaming at each other at one-thirty, and then have to get up and go to work two hours later?

But, citizens though we were of the same household, a vast distance stood between Patricia's life and mine, a chasm not to be bridged by the girders of rational argument. Her pretty, worn face, her tobacco-roughened voice, the astounding question—at some point during those few minutes I began to see that, to Patricia, Allston was most likely a stopping-off place on the way to something worse, not something better. There would be no somber, analytical, all-night talks with her boyfriend on the nature of psychological inheritance and karmic burdens, no dreamy drives past the old Houghton Mifflin building on Park Street. Drug-dealing neighbors, blue strobes on the window shades, landlords who disconnected their telephones and left you to freeze over President's Day Weekend—real as those things were to Amanda and me, they were real to Patricia on a more elemental level. Going before a judge meant something to her that it could not possibly mean to someone, like me, who had always been at the shoulder end of the law's hard arm, and while I had succeeded in finally getting her attention with the court order, I had also, by going to the authorities in that way, crossed a line which she saw very clearly and I had not seen at all.

Even now, I do not know exactly how to describe that line, except to say that it marks some more profound distinction than that between rich and poor, or educated and uneducated. It is part of the invisible barrier that stands between the mind of the slumlord and the mind of his tenant; between those people for whom the great societal machinery of Law and Finance seems benign and helpful, and those for whom it carries the countenance of oppression. I must have seen a reflection of that countenance on Patricia's face that afternoon. My ability to see it, finally, to really see it, was a kind of compensation for the months of debt, scabies, Micronesian infection, bruised lips, broken sleep, and twelve-hour workdays. I had scraped one layer of comfort from my life; in some way, partially, imperfectly, I had grown a more sensitive soul.

It seems to me now that living as Amanda and I lived in Allston, choosing freedom over money, was our clumsy way of trying, to shed—for a little while, when we were young enough and strong enough to do so—a kind of blindness and deafness brought on by our middle-class upbringing and upper-class education. Without knowing it, we wanted to feel a little of what Patricia and thirty million other Patricias felt. We wanted not simply to turn out to be two more nickel-chasers driving down the road toward greater and greater comfort, greater isolation and ease, an ever surer sense that we were simply entitled to whatever good things happened to us.

Perhaps it sounds like the worst kind of falseness and slumming—condescending, sentimental, immature—and maybe that's all it was. But in 1978, in Allston, we were stubborn, idealistic, judgmental, well-enough-intentioned twenty-somethings, carried along by our urges and intuitions, and by a value system—unseasoned, inconsistent, but sincere—that assured us it was better to be the cab-washer than the owner of the company, the tenant than the landlord, to solve things on our own if possible, face to face, rather than letting society's great impersonal institutions solve them for us.

And so we worked it out with Patricia. I promised to walk back down to the courthouse and cancel the order the next day, if she would try harder not to wake us in the middle of the night. And for the remaining few months that we lived in adjoining rooms, Patricia, Amanda, and I cohabited in relative peace.

In the Presence of Goodness

It seems to me that traveling is a spiritual educa-
tion—that is its real purpose. And spiritual educations always have a sting to them.

For the month of April of the Jubilee Year of the Roman Catholic Church, my wife, Amanda, my mother, Eileen, my two-year-old daughter, Alexandra, and I lived in a
rented apartment in Monteverde Nuovo, a residential section of Rome that most tourists never see. The decision to
make this trip, like much of the traveling Amanda and I
have done together, was utterly foolish. We did not have
enough money to go to Rome for a month. We did not
even have enough money to go to Rome for a week. In
fact, we did not really have enough money to get on the
airplane and fly across the ocean. But the idea of going to
Italy came to us in the middle of the winter, when western
Massachusetts—where we'd settled after some wander-
ing—is a gray cold place, and the more we joked about it,
the more we studied guidebooks, and consulted friends,
the more sense it made to spend April there rather than

here. It was not long before the trip began to take on a momentum of its own, familiar to us from other foolish trips, an inertia that rolls over financial considerations like a double-decker bus over a beetle.

As the winter deepened, the bus kept gathering speed. By chance, it turned out that three different groups of our closest friends were going to be in Italy that spring. Then it turned out that my mother would be able to join us— we have traveled happily together in the past. And then, just when we were getting close to the point where reservations had to be made and the foolishness of the whole thing was becoming painfully clear, and the bank balance was slipping even further toward a single round number, and the winter was losing some of its kick, and western Massachusetts wasn't really seeming so bad after all, just then I received an, e-mail from a friend. The e-mail was headed: "Should I Tempt You With This?" and attached was an advertisement for an apartment rental in Rome. The cost—for Rome, for the month of the Jubilee—was about a quarter of what we'd seen advertised on the Internet. This was a clear signal from the gods of travel: we were supposed to go.

Within the hour I was on the telephone to Italy, talking to an American-born woman with a singsong voice, who said the apartment was on the first floor of the building in which she and her husband lived, that they were saving it for their retirement when they would no longer be able to walk up the four flights of stairs, that she wasn't a landlady by profession and wasn't really out to do more than cover their expenses, that it was on a busy street but set in the back of the house and therefore relatively quiet, that there was room for my mother if she would be willing to sleep on a pull-out sofa, that she might have friends who could find us a crib, that there was a bus stop nearby, and two restaurants within walking distance where one might eat fairly well.

Amanda and I talked about it that night. The next day we made a second phone call, to fine-tune our image of the place (Was there a washing machine? Yes. Could one walk to the historical center of Rome? Not easily, no. Was there a lot of rain there in April? Not especially, but you could never be sure. Were there any playgrounds nearby? Yes, across the street, in the city's largest park, the Pamphili Gardens), waited another two days to convince ourselves we weren't doing anything rash, then sent off a deposit. Soon we were buried in the details of preparation: checking passports, making airplane reservations, studying guidebooks, coordinating arrival and departure dates with the various groups of friends.

A few days before we departed, I landed a magazine assignment that eased the financial pressure somewhat. The momentum was unstoppable now. My mother was packing, Amanda and I had a deck of Italian flashcards on the kitchen table, Alexandra had learned to say, "We're going to Italy!" without having the slightest idea what it meant.

It was a difficult crossing: the three-hour drive to Boston, an unpleasant moment with a stubborn cabdriver there; the long wait at the airport; the endless, sleepless, overnight flight to Switzerland and another long wait in the Zurich airport; the connecting flight to Rome, then more unpleasant moments with another cabdriver, who kept insisting, against our ungrammatical but firm objections, that he could fit all our luggage into the trunk of his very medium-sized sedan. "One of you can hold the baby in your arms," he said, "*Cosi*. Like this."

"We want her in the car seat."

"But the car seat will have to go in the trunk so we can put luggage in the back seat."

"We don't want to do that. And all the luggage won't fit in any case."

"What do you mean, won't fit? Of course it will fit."

"It won't fit. We know. We had the same problem in America and had to get two taxis."

"But there aren't any other taxis available now . . . It will fit. Look, see. It will, I tell you."

And so on.

Finally, the man gave up, pulled out of his trunk the two suitcases he'd managed to squeeze in, and sauntered off with a sour expression, as if each of us had taken a turn kicking him.

After a short wait in front of the terminal, we engaged the services of the driver of a neat blue van, loaded in our luggage, and raced out of the airport toward the Eternal City. Palm trees and broken sections of aqueduct, the klaxons of ambulances and the blinking blue lights of traffic police, ugly blocks of apartment buildings and the low rolling hills—we sped into the center, crawled and sprinted through Rome's alarming display of vehicular theatrics, and stopped finally in front of a pink, stucco, four-story building on Via Vitellia. My three traveling companions hurried inside to have a look at the apartment, but I stayed out in the mild air, moving luggage away from the curb. The luggage did not really need to be moved at that particular moment, but I was held out there by a certain kind of fear. Amanda and I had been badly cheated once, years before, when we'd rented a place in southern France, sight unseen. The woman who rented it to us described it as a "chalet with a view of the ocean," which turned out to be something between gross exaggeration and outright lie. The "chalet" was a trailer home in a trailer park half an hour from Bandol. The net on the tennis court was broken. A thick green scum floated on the surface of the community swimming pool. There was, technically, a view of the ocean, but it was a thirty-mile view to a scratch of blue there between the hills.

So I was nervous about the Monteverde apartment. As the van pulled away and shouts of kids playing soccer reached me from the park across the street, I stood there knee-deep in luggage, tired from twenty hours without sleep, and had a sudden image of the four of us living in a cramped, cold apartment for four weeks, spending all that money, deflating all those hopeful Italian fantasies.

I carried the largest two bags through the front entrance and down a short hallway. Amanda was coming out the door of our new home. I watched her face very carefully and said, "How is it?" and she smiled.

Our American landlady with the singsong voice had two names—Molly and Stacey—one by which she was known in the States, and the other by which she was known in Italy, and an Italian husband named Gino who worked as a tour guide, bore a remarkable resemblance to Salvador Dali, and spoke English like a native. Molly was in her fifties, with gray hair, glasses, and a genuine smile, and she turned out to have told us the truth about the apartment: bedroom, full bath, washing machine, parlor with the pull-out sofa bed, small kitchen, heated sun porch where we could take our meals, and a large fenced-in veranda with a few dozen potted trees and a couple of patio chairs. Tile floors, shelves of paperbacks, bedroom windows that could be closed at night with pleated metal shades.

We brought our bags in and unpacked, walked down the street for a pizza and glasses of not very good white wine, put Alexandra into her crib and set my mother up on the sofa bed, and went to sleep ourselves a short while later expecting to wake up early the next morning and set about living our wonderful Roman vacation.

But early the next morning Alexandra stood up in her crib, said, "There's dirty water in my mouth, Mommy," and vomited all over the front of her pajamas. This had not happened since her infancy. We wrote it off to the un-familiar surroundings, different water and food, but she vomited again a few minutes later, and then a third time before the hour was out. I walked up the block to a phar-macy, spent ten minutes stretching my Italian to its limits trying to explain my daughter's symptoms to an officious woman in a white lab coat, and returned with a concoc-tion that only made Alexandra vomit more. We called

Molly, who gave us the name of an English-speaking doctor. Though it was Saturday, she assured us he'd be in his office, seeing patients. I called, and the doctor listened carefully, then suggested we give her melted ice, a few drops at a time, and perhaps a small amount of very cold Coca-Cola. We fed her the melted ice and she vomited again. We tried very cold Coca-Cola and it was more of the same. She was confused and afraid, and then, increasingly thirsty. Two more phone calls, several more bouts of vomiting, and the doctor said, "You'd better bring her here."

We asked Molly to call a taxi for us—for someone not fluent in Italian, procuring a Roman taxi by phone can be a complicated affair—and when it came, we asked the driver to go as slowly as he could, and then not so slowly. The doctor's office turned out to be all the way over on the opposite side of the city, on the third floor of an ivy-ribboned building on a quiet street. His assistant greeted us at the door and showed us into a waiting room filled with toys Alexandra did not glance at. Pale, exhausted, half asleep, she curled up against her mother's chest, moving her large brown eyes back and forth across our faces as if she were about to leave us forever and wanted to fix them in her memory.

We waited twenty minutes before the doctor motioned us into a small room at the end of a hallway. He was a man of indeterminate age, somewhere between forty and seventy, black hair streaked with gray, watery eyes behind a pair of half-glasses, slightly stooped posture and perfect command of English. He began pressing his fingers into

Alexandra's belly, looking into her mouth and eyes, putting a stethoscope to her chest. She stared at him, barely moved. I waited for him to say the word "hospital," or to nod his head and reach confidently into his medicine cabinet. I waited for some signal that he was competent enough to keep my daughter from drying out and dying.

"Let's try some more cold Coke," he said. "I'll put a cup of it in the refrigerator and when it freezes we'll feed it to her a drop at a time."

We waited in the examining room for the Coke to freeze, while the doctor went to attend to other patients. In half an hour he returned and we fed Alexandra three or four icy drops from a paper cup. Five minutes later she threw it up. By this point it was five o'clock in the afternoon and she hadn't eaten or drunk anything for twenty-four hours. When the doctor stepped out of the room again, I examined the diplomas on his walls, stared at the old-looking scale and the chipped paint on his examination table, the tattered chairs. I held Alexandra and walked around the room with her, made a few sentences of small talk with the Austrian assistant, read a paragraph of an Italian newspaper, paced. An hour went by this way. Two hours. We would feed Alexandra a sip of cold Coke, and she would seem to be holding it down for a while—ten minutes, twenty minutes—then she'd start to cry and throw up on her shirtfront, on the towels we held under her chin, on our hands and clothing. The vomitus had a terrible yellow quality to it, like liquefied lemon drops. "Bile," the doctor said. "Wait here, please. We'll try something else."

When he was gone I said to Amanda, "Do you trust this guy?"

"He seems nice. He seems to know what he's doing."

"Kids die from dehydration," I said.

"I know it."

"One more try and we're taking her to the hospital."

The doctor left the apartment with his bicycle. In a light rain he pedaled to a pharmacy—I find it impossible to picture an American physician doing this on a Saturday evening . . . on any evening—and returned with box of suppositories. Alexandra did not seem to notice when he inserted the suppository. She seemed suspended between wakefulness and sleep, in that awful gray world between illness and grave illness, in that place between what is ordinary if not so, nice, and what is horrible, unthinkable. After another half hour we tried a few more sips of Coke. We waited. A few more sips, another wait. An hour went by, an hour and a half she had held down four teaspoons of liquid now, and seemed to be regaining just the smallest bit of her usual shine.

"Looks like it's working," the doctor said, "but we should watch her carefully. I'm having dinner with an old friend tonight and I'm very late." He scrawled something on a piece of paper. "Here's the number of the restaurant. Don't hesitate to call me if she gets worse again, but I think she's going to be fine now."

We had been in his office four hours and twenty minutes. He had ridden out on his bicycle, in the rain, to get medicine. He'd asked us to call him at the restaurant, or at home if need be, no matter what the hour. His fee was seventy-five dollars. He did not take credit cards. We did not have enough Italian money to pay him and pay for the cab home. "Just come by tomorrow or the next day and pay me then," he said, and he went off to his dinner, and, relieved and grateful to the point of giddiness, we went off to ours. He called our apartment that night, just before midnight, and seemed pleased as an uncle when we told him Alexandra was fine.

Amanda and I had been to Rome on two earlier occasions, once for a few hours and once, with my mother, for a few days, but this time we made a point of seeing the historical center of the city from one end to the other. We were overwhelmed and amazed. That there should be such a concentration of beauty in one place—beautiful paintings, beautiful sculptures, magnificent architecture; that so much history remained alive there, for the seeing, for the touching; that the people—most of them—retained their sense of humor, dignity, and an instinctive graciousness while dealing with a perpetual flood of tourists; that they could drive the way they drove and live to laugh about it.

I was nervous about the driving. In fact, before the magazine assignment came through, I had been hoping to avoid renting a car altogether. But the assignment was for a golf magazine, and, with one exception, the golf courses were all located out in the suburbs, so, before leaving Massachusetts, we'd rented a car over the Internet.

The day after our adventure in the doctor's office, I

took a bus from Via Vitellia to the center of the city, then tried, to find the rental office on foot and ended up walking in a large circle. Map in hand, I tried again, striding along Rome's labyrinthine streets and alleys past clumps of tourists staring at churches, and women talking to each other through thousand-year-old windows above my head. Pigeons and cats, couples on bicycles, horn blasts, squealing tires, buzzing motorbikes, stucco walls and shuttered doorways, plane trees with their mottled bark, and the palpable sense that, for millennia, people had walked these same alleys and crossed these same streets, carrying with them their tiny individual dramas.

There was the river again. I had made another circle. I walked three more blocks then raised my arm in surrender and took a taxi to the rental office, where, after signing my name a few dozen times, I was given the keys to a white four-door car, diesel-powered, made by the company that makes Range Rovers.

Driving a Rover sedan in Rome is the rough equivalent of driving a Humvee in Manhattan. It is too large by half for the narrow streets, too difficult to maneuver. Add in the grumbling engine, the stick shift, and fleets of crazy Romans on motor scooters, motorcycles, and behind the wheels of tiny, quick automobiles, and you have a prescription for madness.

But my cab driving experience in Boston turned out to be fair preparation for the streets of Rome, and by following the river and sneaking behind the Vatican, consulting the map at stoplights, pounding my horn and pushing my fenders into the smallest openings in imitation of the people I saw around me, I managed to make it back to Via Vitellia in one piece. Finding a parking space, however, proved to be an adventure. Finding one, and then turning into it across a lane of manic motorcyclists and aggressive truck drivers—two adventures.

In possession of a set of wheels now, healthy and un-packed, truly settled in, we fell into a regular routine. First thing in the morning I would walk around the corner to a little convenience store where a kind, quiet woman with sad eyes sold just-baked brioches, sweet rolls, and jelly-filled croissants for 1,000 lire each. I'd carry the warm pa-per bag back to the apartment. Amanda and my mother would brew coffee, squeeze the juice of blood oranges in-to Molly's irregular assortment of glasses, set out cereal and fruit, and we'd sit in the heated, glassed-in porch and have our leisurely breakfast.

After breakfast, on days when I wasn't scheduled to play golf, we'd load ourselves into the Rover, Alexandra strapped into her car seat in back next to my mother, Amanda and I in front, and drive up across the Janiculum Hill, down through the tangled traffic of Trastevere, across the Tiber and into the city proper. Somehow, we always found a place to park. Often this was an illegal place—too close to the corner of an intersection, partially blocking the fence of a construction site—but that did not seem to matter to the other drivers we saw doing the same thing, and did not seem to matter very much to the police: we never returned to find a ticket on the windshield.

Each day we explored a different section of the city— sometimes going only as far as the Janiculum Hill (just up the road from our apartment), with its panoramic views of Rome's low, dun-colored skyline, its puppet shows and carousel, its stands selling gelati and cotton candy. There would be an excursion to the Aventine Hill with its ancient churches and patches of greenery and quiet; to the winding old streets of the Jewish Ghetto; the graceful side hill twist of Via Veneto with glamorous women sipping espresso at sidewalk cafes and tourists buying calendars in bookshops; or the churches, small restaurants, and wine-tasting shops of Trastevere, the old working-class neighborhood that has now turned into a hangout for Italian movie stars and begging Gypsy children; or the grandeur and crowds at the Vatican; or the tree-lined lanes of the Borghese Gardens; or the Protestant cemetery with its graves of Keats and Shelley and its legions of wild cats.

The Trevi Fountain, the Spanish Steps, the Coliseum and Forum and the intricate brick ruins of the Baths of Caracalla, one spectacular church after the next—on side streets, in piazzas, hidden behind plain-looking wooden doors that did not quite close. Inside these churches—some of which were empty in midday, even in the high season for Catholic tourism—we would find Caravaggios hanging on the walls, apses painted by Peter Paul Rubens or designed by Leonardo da Vinci, the preserved bodies of saints, flickering votive candles, elaborate mosaics, marble pillars as thick around as a small sequoia and twice as old. My mother is a devout Catholic and I am a devout Buddhist with deep Catholic roots and Amanda is a former Congregationalist with Buddhist leanings, but the spiritual power of those places crossed all religious lines. There were millions of hours of handwork in them, generations of labor and sweat; and the dignity and brilliance of all that effort could not be dimmed by time. We would pray for family at home, or just try to settle our minds after the frenzy of the road, while Alexandra knocked between pews and made her voice echo up against paintings of the Christ-child and his mother and their friends.

On each of these excursions we walked miles and miles, stopping every couple of hours for cappuccino (which the Italians drink only in the morning, and tourists drink all day long), or a plate of *penne amatriciana*, or *spaghetti bolognaise*, or *linguini alle vongole*, at a restaurant we'd never seen before. And when the day was finished we fought our way back through the madness of the road, squeezed into a parking space on Via Vitellia, and passed a quiet evening at home.

And home was what Monteverde Nuovo began to feel like. Amanda stocked the cabinets with food, and cooked pasta with peas or pork chops with broccoli or hamburgers with fresh spears of asparagus on the side. Alexandra made a friend in the playground. The woman at the convenience store greeted me with a smile. Molly and Gino stopped by to see that we had settled in well. We learned the best places to buy diesel fuel with a credit card and the best routes into and out of the city and the best ways to look for parking spaces and the best supermarket. We began to establish a presence there, among the women with their shopping bags, and teenagers with their Walkmans, and men in polished shoes.

Twice a week I drove out into the suburbs to play golf.

I made a few friends that way, too, joining up with better and less good players on the course, stopping after nine holes for a lunch of fresh-grilled meat, fresh salad greens, the coarse Roman bread that is served without butter and dipped in extra virgin olive oil, a bowl of fresh fruit and sometimes a glass of wine or a few sips of heavily sugared espresso. On those days, Amanda, Alexandra, and my mother would stroll the quiet lanes of the Pamphili Gardens across the street, bumping into other Americans with kids, shooting rolls of film, watching old men play cards and teenagers kiss on park benches. It was a nice life we were making for ourselves there, in the Italian sun. It was what traveling is supposed to be.

But there is a trick that travelers play—on themselves and on others. The trick entails pretending—to themselves and to others—that by setting out on the road they somehow automatically leave behind all the mundane aspects of living, the stretches of sour mood, the arguments and frustrations, the burps of bad luck that echo through any given week at home.

There is some truth to it. There is a way in which we leave a part of ourselves behind whenever we embark on a long trip. So much of our time is taken up with work and errands that traveling automatically frees up a sector of our attention, lets us breathe, look around, appreciate the deep mystery and quick miracle of our own existence.

But the tricks we try to play never really work. In the gray cold evenings in Massachusetts, we had imagined Rome as sunny and spectacular: unrivaled meals, gracious natives, a deep, pleased peace that lasted from the moment we climbed out of bed to the moment we climbed back in.

There were, indeed, flashes of that peace. I remember, for instance, sitting at a table in a Sardinian restaurant in Trastevere. Good friends from Vermont were sitting opposite us, the waiter was pinching Alexandra's cheeks and sneaking her pieces of candy, the cooks were making jokes in the kitchen, there was a good bottle of white wine on the table next to a stack of unleavened Sardinian bread, Amanda rested her hand on my thigh, and my mother was smiling and talking with our friends' lovely daughter. And after a long, pleasant meal we walked out into a clear spring night with darkness just falling and the trolleys humming along on their tracks and the faces of the old buildings sinking into soft shadows broken by squares of yellow light.

Moments like that are compensation for everything— for the expense, the sleepless night on Swissair, the traffic mania. They embed themselves in the memory of the ardent traveler. They lure you back.

But there are other moments, too. Some are tiny aggravations—the wheel on your child's stroller falls off halfway up the Aventine Hill on a hot morning. Or you encounter a crabby clerk in a stationery store; or, guidebook in hand, make the unnerving drive across the metropolis hoping to see a particular museum, only to find that the museum is closed for repairs that week. It rains when you had a picnic planned. Or the *spaghetti al mare* in a promising new restaurant is drenched in butter and oil, the bread slightly stale, the prices high, and your daughter won't sit still no matter what strategies her parents or her grandmother resort to.

Some are less than beautiful aspects of yourself, ugly little pieces of private psychology that you can somehow keep under wraps in Massachusetts. The mild, constant strain of living away from home pulls the curtain away from them. You snarl at your spouse or your mother after a poor night's sleep, you have a spasm of self-consciousness while walking onto an exclusive golf course and feel like a much younger version of yourself, you curse the traffic, find yourself immersed in a selfish fantasy of traveling alone, stopping when you want to stop, eating where you want to eat, spending or not spending as the mood strikes you.

Without the distraction of work, these moments take on, by some dark magic, a weight you've never known them to have at home. They bear down on you, shadowing the day. You're not supposed to have bad moods in Italy, you're not supposed to argue with your wife, what's wrong with you? You're supposed to be here having a good—a perfect—time, and instead you're upset. And what about all this money you're spending? And so on.

There is no perfect place, no perfect self. Everyone knows that. And yet the dreams of travelers—and sometimes the accounts of travel writers—are lined with this imagined perfection, as if, though we know it can't possibly be true, we nevertheless cling to the fantasy that, in Italy, in Rome, we will string together thirty unblemished days, pull our finer self out of a suitcase, banish lousy moods, domestic arguments, toothaches, and find our selves surrounded by people who are overjoyed to see us, who love and admire our daughter as we love and admire her.

My suspicion is that what we are really doing when we envision a vacation in this way is imagining our finest self. Of course it is not possible to follow the perfect meal with the perfect lovemaking with the perfect night's sleep with the perfect cappuccino and brioche for breakfast with a trip to the perfectly designed church, and so on. We can touch this externally generated perfection for moments at a time, perhaps even a full day at a time now and again, but, in spite of what the advertising agencies would have us believe, we cannot hold it.

Perhaps, though, we do have the potential for holding on to the state of mind. I have known people who seem to hold it—not a continuous ecstasy so much as a continuous calm, which strikes me as preferable. My father's mother was one of those people. I have seen stretches of it in Amanda and my mother, and felt them in myself. Maybe the purpose of travel—of any vacation—is to feed us flashes of this interior joy so that we can then go home and attempt to maintain it through the illnesses and monotony, the triumphs and tragedies of everyday existence.

I think sometimes that we all secretly sense we have the capability of cultivating that kind of inner steadiness. I believe at times that Amanda and I are drawn to travel and to dream about traveling because we have some intuitive faith that, by freeing ourselves from the duties and familiar pleasures of home, we will be shown—in Rome, in

Mexico, on a beach at Cape Cod—flashes of a profound calm, an appreciation, that we might nurture in more familiar places. We imagine we will find, on the road, what is actually already in us—a species of goodness that is as natural as breath.

For some of us, that interior calm needs an exterior kick-start, and, over the last ten years, the most reliable kick-start has become, for Amanda and me, a trip to Italy. The food, the language, the beautiful buildings, the sense of history, the warmth of the people—all of it combines with the absence of our domestic duties to work a kind of spell on us. Our friends buy furniture when they have extra money, or invest it for their retirement, or just enjoy the feeling of having a financial cushion. We go to Italy. We don't know exactly why. It makes us happy. Even with all the aggravations of the road, it makes us happy.

For me, some of this happiness comes from the fact that being around Italians reminds me of the best moments of my childhood. We lived either upstairs from, or next door to, my father's parents, Joseph and Eleonora Merullo, who'd come to America from small villages east of Naples, settled near Boston and raised eight children there. Those children married and had children of their own, and all of that crowd—my parents, paternal grandparents, the fourteen aunts and uncles and twenty-five cousins on my father's side—gathered in my grandparents' backyard every Sunday of my childhood. It would take an entire book to recount the feelings of those days, the physical affection and sense of unity, the laughter and games and meals. Sometimes, in Italy, the pure joy of that time returns to me in unexpected flashes. I was sitting in a restaurant in the Dolomites once, in a town called Cavalese, waiting to be served, when a crowd of people came through the door—a large family—and the way they were talking to each other and the smells from the kitchen—all of it fell upon my senses like a sweet dusting from the past. I looked up at them, and it was as if forty years had fallen away and I were looking up from the happiest feelings of childhood, from the sense of belonging, and being loved without question, the sense that there was an unending, wonderful future spreading out in front of this little sparkling gem of a present moment.

Everyone contributed to the joy and warmth of those gatherings, the sense of love that ran through that large family. But there was a mysterious way in which my grandmother stood at the center of it—all the surviving Merullos acknowledge that. She had been a pretty girl in her youth, but was heavy and rather plain by the time I knew her. There was nothing especially notable about her personality either: in a crowd at wakes or weddings, she would blend into the background with her hands folded in front of her and her patent-leather purse dangling from her wrists. She spent most of her life cooking, cleaning, and raising children. But there was a certain quiet light always shining through her, a generosity of spirit, an enormous capacity for love. My mother—who raised her children within earshot of her mother-in-law—talks about it often. People who are not part of the family talk about it. To the extent that it is possible in a human being, she was without ego, without agenda, without harsh judgments, without selfishness. Stepping into her kitchen, her domain, you felt yourself to be in the presence of goodness.

So, as if to honor her, or as if to try and touch that goodness again, Amanda, my mother, and I decided that, rather than fighting the mobs in Saint Peter's Square on Easter Sunday, we would drive south to the village where my grandmother had been born, and celebrate the holiday there.

Two nights before we were supposed to leave on that trip-within-a-trip, Molly and Gino invited us upstairs for dinner. It was a warm April Thursday, almost summerish, and we sat crowded into their kitchen while the two of them took turns putting together a meal of grilled chicken, risotto, and fresh fennel salad. There was good wine and bread and—as was also the case in the apartment downstairs—the walls were hung with Molly's delicate ink drawings, but what put the shine on the evening for me was the naturalness of their hospitality. A genuine affection curled around the little table, as if they understood instinctively that we were plain people, people full of quirks and flaws and ribboned here and there with obvious but inconsequential insecurities; people who carried no enormous egos or buried angers; people like themselves. For a couple of hours on that warm night, we were able to scrape away the surface differences and make some basic, human-to-human connection. Gino's knowledge of the history of Rome and its treasures was encyclopedic. Mixing the fennel and oil, making coffee, he treated us to mini-lectures on the evolution of certain neighborhoods and the intricacies of the city's cuisine, architecture, and dialect. And near the end of the evening he said, "Would it be possible for you to meet me downstairs tomorrow at seven o'clock in the morning?"

"It would be possible. Alexandra is usually up by then. Why?"

"Because I have a free hour tomorrow at the beginning of the day. I can give you a private—or at least an almost private—showing of the Sistine Chapel. Is this something you would like?"

At quarter to eight the next morning—Good Friday— Gino led us down the long corridors of the Vatican Museum, down a short set of steps, and through a door into the Capella Sistina. There were five other people inside—a couple, two children, and a guide whose voice echoed against the ceiling. Gino stayed with us a few minutes, pointing out certain details, then had to leave to meet a group of English tourists outside, and for the next three-quarters of an hour we and the other family had that remarkable room to ourselves. Amanda, my mother, and I took turns corralling Alexandra as she raced across the tile floor with a newfound Italian boyfriend. The rest of the time we just stood there, moving our eyes over the ceiling and walls, staring at the faces and bodies, taking in what might be described as the entirety of the psychological possibilities of human nature, there in paint on stone.

The pastels on the ceiling, the musculature of the saints and sinners, the overarching theme of divisiveness

in life—night from day, good from bad, man from woman
—it seemed to me that Michelangelo had taken all that
and somehow made us see the unity in it, as if he were
God, or God's stand-in, and had spun multiplicity from a
molecule. There were so many places to look, so much to
try to absorb, but beyond that there was a larger sense of
the whole of the masterwork: it was enough just to be
there, without knowing what everything signified, without
believing or disbelieving that his work bore any real relationship to the story of the creation of the world.

There was some kind of otherworldly presence
there—God, spirituality, an extraordinary artistic genius—
and it seemed to me to concentrate itself in a few images
on the forward wall. These were the faces of the saved,
hovering very close to, but still separated from, their fu-
rious creator. Though they had escaped the fate of the
souls below them, been brought up into the eternal bliss
of God's presence for all time, though they had been
judged good, once and for all and forever, their faces
showed not joy, but awe and tribulation. Some of them
could not even look at God. Others seemed to be sneaking a quick glance, still worried, perhaps, about a late-in-
the-game divine change of mind. I kept my eyes on them
until we could hear the throngs of tourists tramping down
the hall, and then feel people spilling into the room—
Belgians, Japanese, Ger mans, Canadians—and the unex-
pectedness of those expressions seemed to me the most
marvelous part of Michelangelo's achievement. There, in
paint on stone, he had captured the essence of the human
predicament: existential helplessness armored by a thin

thin shell of ability and conceit; the awful paradox of feeling a natural drive toward goodness, and a simultaneous resistance to it; the ache for selflessness and the draw of desire; the intimation that there is some higher, better, truer state available to us, and the sense that we cannot quite reach it, on some days not even imagine it.

Former Catholic that I am, it has long seemed to me that the account of Christ's crucifixion and resurrection contain all our confused motivations, all the different selves that compete behind our "I." There is Pontius Pilate, presented with the ultimate choice between right and wrong, and failing to find the courage in himself to make a decision. There is the mob screaming for a murderer to be released and a spiritual teacher to be crucified. There are the little acts of kindness and courage—Simon helping Christ carry the cross—in the midst of a maelstrom of self-interest. Somewhere in my twenties the list of rules put forth by the Roman Catholic Church became too long for me, the laws too arbitrary, some of the attitudes too narrow, harsh, and un-Christlike. But the power of the biblical stories remained, and remains still, and the days leading up to Easter occupy a special place in my spiritual landscape. And so, seeing Michelangelo's masterwork on Good Friday was a little bit like a second baptism for me, a reminder, as one Buddhist teacher puts it, to "make my mind big."

In Italy the Monday and Tuesday after Easter are holidays, so on Friday and Saturday—start of the four-day weekend—the highways are clogged with people leaving the city. We got a fairly late start on Saturday morning and made it as far as the Ring Road (in Italian it has a much prettier name: *Il Grande Raccordo Annulare*) without much trouble. We even traveled along the *Annulare* two or three exits, moving south and east, before the full magnitude of the holiday exodus became apparent.

Somewhere not far from the exit for the Naples autostrada, traffic on the four-lane highway thickened like gravy being reduced on a stove. We went from seventy miles an hour to seven. We crawled along, reached the exit, crept up the ramp onto the first stretches of the road south, then came to a full stop. After five minutes we rolled forward a few car lengths, then stopped dead a second time. There was a bank of toll booths off in the distance, and eventually, when we crested a rise, we could see two thick lines of cars feeding onto the highway from the left, and what seemed like thousands of stalled vehicles in front of us. Judging from the expressions of passengers in the cars pressing in on either side, there was nothing unusual about the situation. They chatted on cell phones, gazed out the window, leaned their heads slightly toward each other in two, three, or four-way conversations.

I believe it took us just under an hour to reach the toll booth, a distance of less than two miles. Beyond the toll, the traffic freed up a bit, but even then we and our neighbors would glide steadily forward for a few dozen kilometers at something approaching normal speed, then suddenly slow down almost to a stop and inch along for ten or fifteen minutes. Two hours after leaving Via Vitellia, we had gone sixty miles, about 40 percent of the way to my grandmother's village. It was time for lunch.

We left the highway at the exit for Cefalu, asked a pedestrian or two where we might find a wholesome meal, and ended up at a tourist hotel where we had a small feast—pasta and the *tavola calda*, or warm table. The *tavola* in the hotel dining area was set in the center of a large sunny room and covered with dishes of food. There were grilled peppers, zucchini, summer, squash, pickled mushrooms, eggplant parmigiana, balls of mozzarella, asparagus in oil, chickpeas, fennel, carrots, artichoke hearts, sardines, olives, pecorino, cooked cauliflower heads the size of golf balls, tortes, custards, and cakes of all description. The *tavola calda* resembles the salad buffet in an American restaurant in something like the way that a Black Angus filet mignon grilled over a mesquite fire resembles a decent hamburger. We made up plates and carried them to the table, the slow woes of the highway forgotten. We slathered butter on the coarse, salty bread, poured out glasses of cold mineral water, and wine, pushed the vegetables aside when the pasta arrived, ordered cappuccino to keep us awake for the rest of the ride south, followed our energetic Alexandra out onto the porch, where there was a set of swings, and an Italian brother and sister about her own age.

After a respite of over an hour we were back on the road, the traffic moving more freely now, the day growing warmer with every kilometer we traveled south. Alexandra slept. My mother remarked on the scenery: sharp green and gray hills rising and falling away to the east, pockets of stucco and concrete houses in the valley to our right, the occasional fortified city on top of a hill, its four-hundred-year-old houses clustered close together, their windows looking out and down on green fields and grazing land, on a highway sparkling with the reflected sunlight from thousands of windshields.

In the restaurant it had occurred to me, belatedly, that since it was a holiday weekend, we might have trouble finding a hotel room—even in the quiet cities near my grandmother's village. On a previous visit, Amanda and I had stayed in the only nearby hotel, in the small city of Atripalda. I remembered the name of the hotel, and with the help of the clerk at the desk, found the number in her directory, called, and made myself understood. Solidly booked. We tried another place, booked up too. On the third try I found an opening and reserved a room. Amanda had the directions written down now on a scrap of paper. We turned off the Naples autostrada onto the one for Benevento, where the hills were green and steep, reminding us of parts of Switzerland. We found the exit, located the driveway up to the hotel. But when I went in to check out the room I found tight quarters smelling strongly of disinfectant, and when the owner told me there was a nightclub downstairs and there might be a little noise—*un po' di rumore,* I apologized, said it wasn't right for us, and with some misgivings broke the reservation and returned to the car with the bad news.

We decided to just drive to the village—Parolise (Padohleesay), it is called—make a quick tour while there was still light enough to see it, and take our chances finding a motel nearby. This is the traditional approach Amanda and I use in finding lodging. We have used it all over the world, from New Hampshire to the Yucatan, from Edinburgh to Bavaria, and it has resulted in some wonderful surprises – a room with a balcony overlooking Lago di Garda in northern Italy, a chalet with a view of the Alps near Salzburg. And it has resulted in some awful late-night drives through dark hinterlands, passing one NO VACANCY sign after the next, and ending up in a fleabag of a place with no toilet seats and holes in the screens on the windows.

But it was still only late afternoon. What was the worst that could happen?

Parolise is a tiny piece of the province of Campagna. You can walk from one end of it to the other in eight minutes. The countryside around it is rolling and green (at least in spring: I remember it as dusty brown from our earlier visit, in summer), with mostly modern homes pocking the hillsides. You can turn into it from a small two-lane highway bridge and then climb gently into the center of town. There you pass a small bakery, one of three commercial establishments. At the bakery, make a very sharp right onto a cobblestone street, then, immediately, a left, and climb a steep hill that feeds into the town square. There is a church at one end of this small, flat square, a yellowish building that seems to be tilting to one side. Next to it on the left are some three-story brick houses still showing damage from the 1980 earthquake. The other sides of the square—which measures forty yards across in both directions—are fronted by newer, two-story homes, gray and tan, with balconies and no front yards.

We pulled the grumbling white Rover up into the square and parked. "The churchbells are going to ring," Alexandra said to my mother. A moment later they did.

While Amanda was getting out some of her photography equipment, and my mother was helping Alexandra undo the buckles on her car seat, I noticed a group of children and two women sitting on a stoop, and went across the square to practice my Italian on them. "*Buona sera*," I said, and when they responded in a friendly enough fashion I told them we were from America, and that my grandmother had been born here in this *paese* a hundred and fifteen years earlier. The women smiled, made small exclamations of surprise. I asked them if there was hotel nearby where we might stay, because we wanted to attend Easter mass the next morning, here, in this church.

"The Hotel Christopher in Atripalda," one of the women said in Italian.

"I tried it. It's full. Is there another one not too far away?"

One woman looked at the other, glanced at the people getting out of the Rover, and said. "You can stay in my house."

"No, there's four of us."

"We'll move the children out and into my friend's house here, and you can have the whole house to yourselves."

"Move the children out? We couldn't."

My three traveling companions came up and we introduced ourselves. "They invited us to stay in their house tonight," I said to Amanda. "They're going to move out and give us the house to ourselves."

"We couldn't do that."

But it turned out that we could. There were eleven children in the group on the front step. Two of them—girls probably fifteen and eleven—led us across the square, down a short set of steps with views of the hills to the west, and into a rambling building. More children followed. We were being given a tour of the house—there must have been ten rooms, and the kids were pulling open drawers and closets and gathering up their Easter clothes in their arms. "You can sleep here," the main guide, a beautiful eleven-year-old named Marina, was telling us. "Or here. Your mother can sleep here. Here's the crib, where Alessandria can sleep."

We followed them in a daze.

"Here's one bathroom for your mother. Here's a bathroom for you. Here's the kitchen and here's where we keep the cereal, and the tea. Do you drink coffee in the morning? Here's the coffee, and bread."

"You all live here?"

"Yes."

"How many?"

"Nine. Nine children and Gilda, the woman who was with us. It's a *Casa Zattera*," the fifteen-year-old said. I did not know the word.

"And you're all going to move out?"

"Yes. We'll stay at Carmelina's. She has two children there. We like to stay there."

It would be untrue to say that when I walked across the square toward the group of children and women, I expected them to offer us a place to stay. I didn't expect that. I didn't ask about hotels in a false way, hoping to kick-start the generosity of someone in the group, showing off my cute kid, mentioning my grandmother, making a strategic advance on their good hearts. But it would also be untrue to say that the act of generosity was really foreign and surprising to me. It wasn't. A similar thing had happened to me on Truk, where Samurai and Miako's family had welcomed me into their very modest home—not for a night but for months. And in Moscow, in Siberia, in the dry warm reaches of Uzbekistan—I was invited into hundreds of homes for dinner, usually at the end of a first conversation. Almost without exception the people who invited me were from the poorer working class of Soviets, people who lived in two or at most three rooms—a grandmother, a husband and wife, sometimes one or two children—and spent a week's pay on the meal they offered, and invited me back a second time, and a third. Amanda and I have done things like that ourselves, as has my mother, extending an invitation for a meal or a place to stay to people we did not know but felt, intuitively, were decent people, honest people, people like ourselves. Even in a world made harsher by suspicion and greed, an urge toward hospitality lives on in most of us.

But it is exceedingly difficult to write about this kind of generosity, to write about people like these, to write about the goodness in the human race, without sounding saccharine and inauthentic, without sounding—to a reader and to myself—like those types of people who go around smiling too much, being too obviously kind all the time, as if trying to convince themselves, against all logic and evidence, that the world is a place without any harshness in it, that they are people without any selfishness in them, and that there are no walls between their souls and others'. The only way a writer can convey anything of any worth is to be as honest as he or she knows how to be. Which means scratching around in yourself to find the cancerous cells—the fake optimism, the urge to present yourself as decent or holy or wise or modest, the urge not to convey but to propagandize, to impose your neat view of things on the ragged complexity that is life. I admit, here, to having a mostly positive sense of the way the world is put together. I have seen a bit of evil in my life—you can't live twenty-eight months in the USSR, you can't live anywhere, without seeing a bit of evil—and I have seen some death and suffering, and suffered myself from a series of injuries and afflictions. Those are my credentials, my claims to at least a somewhat seasoned optimism. I admit here that, though I do not claim to be sure, and have a real problem with people who do claim to be sure, it seems to me that some kind of benevolent force runs the universe. I believe this in spite of the torture and misery, the murder and molestation. It is clear enough to me that I may only want the world to be a good place, for life to make sense, and that the motivation for my faith might be wholly selfish. I accept that possibility. I accept the possibility that all my cherished theories about God and the Afterlife and Karma and Enlightenment might turn out to be so much self-delusion, born of the terrible fear of pain, meaningless-ness, and the end of my own existence.

For the writer, for the individual heart, there is a great risk in touching up the world with golden paint and then shining soft light on it.

But there is risk at the other end of the spectrum as well, and it seems to me that the educated mind does not see that risk quite as clearly. There is a danger – spiritual, psychological, emotional, even practical—in being suspi-cious of all goodness, piling up evidence of the meaning-lessness of living, the hard-heartedness of divinity. If fear lies at the root of the saccharine view, then another kind of fear commands the heart of the cynic. The cynic is ter-rified of goodness, and mocks it. The cynic is afraid to be-lieve that human existence aims toward some greater pur-pose—just as the religious fanatic is afraid to believe it doesn't. Yet, to the intellectual, cynicism is somehow a more defensible posture. The cynic guards himself, at all costs, against disappointment, using ridicule to defend himself against ridicule, as if the pain of some childhood wound echoes perpetually in his consciousness. The terri-tory he abides in is a safe but sterile territory, the world he describes to himself a world in which goodness must al-ways be proven false, saints and heroes must be shown to have flaws, and their saintliness and heroism thereby dis-counted, love must be undependable and therefore ulti-mately not real.

It seems to me sometimes that what the Pollyanna and the cynic share is an inability to live with their own speckled nature: the former denies all evil in himself and so tries to deny it in the world; and the latter, so terrified by the existence of his own evil thoughts and selfish urges, cannot admit that there might be pure good, that there might be—in himself and what surrounds him—some evolution, however hidden, uneven, and frightening, toward a better state of being.

I suppose much of my own belief system has its roots in the life of my father's mother. She died when I was twenty-one, so my view of her was not merely a child's view. I lived above her, or beside her, for eighteen years, so my sense of her did not come only from carefully presented moments at happy events. She was not saccharine in her pronouncements about life; she was, in fact, not given to pronouncements of any kind except for the often repeated idea that true happiness was to be found in the relationship between husband and wife. She was not syrupy: I keep a letter on my desk, written in her own hand, in which she chastises her husband, who had found work out of state during the Depression, for seeming inattentiveness (though the letter ends with effusive expressions of love). Her goodness, of which I am convinced beyond a doubt, consisted not of upbeat proclamations and ceaseless smiles, but of a twin sense of selflessness and authenticity. The memory of it resounds in my internal world like a reverse image of the cynic's memories of abuse. I am sure I went to Parolise hoping to refresh that memory, hoping to find traces of her there, hoping, through some traveler's alchemy, to expose my daughter to the spirit of her late great-grandmother.

In an attempt to pay back Gilda and Carmelina and the kids for their generosity, we insisted on taking them all out for supper. They piled into a van, we climbed into our Rover, Carmelina took her own Fiat with a couple of kids in the back. We went halfway down the familiar road to Atripalda, then turned up the neighboring steep hill and into the driveway of a place called Il Treno, which looked like a couple of train cars that had been abandoned in a dusty vacant lot.

Somehow there—this happens to me with uncanny frequency—I found myself drawn into conversation with a complete stranger. The children were running and playing in the Treno's dusty yard, Amanda and my mother were talking with Carmelina and Gilda, I walked up the wooden ramp that led to the door, saw a man standing there, said hello in Italian, got a response in Cockney English, and was caught up in twenty minutes of one of the most bizarre conversations I have ever held. The man told me his sister owned the restaurant, and he was in Italy "on a little business." When, after another few exchanges, I asked him what line of work he was in he said, "Oh just a little something . . . you could say it was the security business."

"You need security here, at this place?"

"Not here. It's a sort of, you could say, private security business."

"Here, in Italy? Are you a bodyguard?"

"All over the world, we work, wherever there's a need. We've even been called in to do a little job in your White House."

"Do you work for a government?"

"Let's just say we work for someone who is higher than government. A businessman. A very very big businessman."

"Are you an assassin?"

"We do what needs to be done. We're trained to do things very quickly and quietly. You might see me in town tonight and you'd think I was a bum. I'd be dressed like a bum, I'd act like a bum. But when the time came to act we would act without hesitation. If we have to get rid of some people for the good of, humanity, a very very big drug dealer, say, well, we'd do that, but no one would ever know. The person would just disappear, that's all."

"You must get paid a great deal."

"I have no need of money. None of us do. Let's just say that when I'm done with this work, in a year or twenty years, I'll have a fantastic house given to me anywhere in the world I want it, and I'll never have to worry about money again.

"Do you get paid now?"

"Not in the usual sense of getting paid, no. Let's just say everything I need is given to me, taken care of."

"Have you ever worked in Russia?"

"The Russians are the hardest people to work with. We've done a few jobs there, it isn't very pleasant."

"Do you speak other languages?"

"We have inside people who do that part of it. We just get called in for a very very specific job, and then we're out again in a matter of hours."

I was being called into the restaurant. Slightly un-

169

nerved, I shook the man's hand—as muscled and hard as the rest of him—and went in to pizza, a mixed green salad, wine, and dessert in an old railroad wagon with table cloths, the smell of Italian cooking, and booths filled with teasing, pinching, curious kids who came, it turned out, from families torn apart by poverty, addiction, and abuse. An hour later, when I went to one end of the car to pay the bill, the assassin's sister took 20 percent off the total because we were there with the kids from Casa Zattera.

Zattera means "raft" in Italian. The home in which we spent the night was owned by the Italian government, and used to house children who'd been taken away from extremely unhealthy family situations. At that moment there were nine kids in Gilda's care. The youngest was a seventeen-month-old boy named Nicolo, and the eldest two fifteen-year-old girls named Suzanna and Marta. The children were so well behaved, the house so clean, that it seemed impossible they'd come from terrible backgrounds, except that every now and then in the face of one of them, in an unguarded moment, you'd see the weariness of an adult, a trail of pain and hurt leading back into the not very distant past. But most of the time they were just children. They buzzed around Alexandra like so many bees, holding her, talking to her, laughing with her. They treated my mother and me and Amanda with a sort of bemused reverence, taking my mother by the hand and applying their own makeup to her eyelids and cheeks. And they treated Gilda as if she were both sister and mother at once. Sister and mother and savior, perhaps.

The next morning we did, in fact, attend mass in the church where my father's mother must have worshipped in the last years of the nineteenth century, when she was a teenage girl. The interior of the building was small and plain compared to what we'd seen in Rome: flowers on the altar and a few dozen provincial families in their Easter best. Carmelina strummed the guitar for a small choir that included her own two foster children and several of Gilda's. An old woman with a crooked finger and an unfriendly air sat beside us in the pew and scolded Alexandra whenever she climbed down or twisted back and forth, or did any of the other things two-year-olds do when asked to stay in one place for more than sixty seconds at a time. Amanda and I and my mother took turns holding baby Nicolo during the service, to give Gilda a short reprieve, and she accepted this favor naturally, without thanking us. The priest went through the ancient ritual of the mass, reciting prayers, blessing the water and wine, handing out the Eucharistic wafers. We took photographs afterwards on the little square in front of the church. We strolled a loop through Parolise. We went back to the house, where the children broke open the football-sized chocolate eggs that mean Easter Sunday for Italian kids, and let Alexandra break one open, and let her keep the little plastic prize inside. We had coffee and cake and exchanged addresses, hugged and kissed, then piled our things back into the Rover and made the long hot drive back to Rome.

Sometimes now, I think about Gilda and Carmelina and their kids at the strangest times: when I am headed

171

out for a game of golf, or writing a monthly payment check on my new car, or when Alexandra shrieks and demands something at dinner or suns happily across the lawn. Gilda was an attractive, dark-haired woman, Swiss by birth, fluent in Italian and nearly fluent in English. "I have no more room, no more energy," she told Amanda, "but when I hear of another case I can't seem to say no. That's how he came here." She gestured toward the baby. "It's peaceful hear today, but you should see them sometimes. Sometimes it's like a war in this house."

During our short visit, I watched her, and Carmelina, as if watching a rare specimen of animal I'd heard about but never encountered in the field. I saw her get angry once – at Matteo when he dashed out in front of the car after mass. And I saw her teasing and joking with one of the teenage girls, grabbing her arms then stepping back out of reach, as if they were both in the ninth grade. At Il Treno she let herself relax for a moment, sipping from a glass of wine with the baby beside her asleep in the booth and her friend Carmelina sitting opposite. But most of the time she seemed to me a semi-visible figure, as if her own dreams and urges had been so deeply buried that she no longer had any need to look at herself or pile up pleasures on all sides to hold her erect. Often, in the past, when I had encountered people doing work like the work Gilda was doing – there had been a strident quality about them, almost as if they were angry at the world for not being a better place, at others for not sharing the load or at least realizing the size of the load that had to be shared. But, like my father's mother – whose presence seemed so

palpable during that service in that plain little church –
Gilda was almost invisible, there and not there at once,
perhaps too tired for stridency or anger, perhaps too
good. How strange it was that we should meet her, in Parolise of all places, on Easter Sunday, in front of a house
past which my grandmother must have walked a thousand
times. She had been born, it turned out, on the same day
as Alexandra, December 17. She owned a dog, it turned
out, with the same name as my mother's dog Ben. Her
friend Carmelina, it turned out, had been born and baptized in America, and her godfather lived in Revere, where
I had been born and raised, where my mother still lived.
How strange it all was.

Not long ago we sent off a small check and asked Gilda to take all the kids to Il Treno, on us, which made me
feel something like the way I felt when I reached out to
her during the mass and took the baby from her arms, and
held him for fifteen or twenty minutes then passed him on
to my mother. I won't say it was the feeling expressed in
the faces of the saved on the Sistine Chapel wall as they
looked at their savior—Gilda was human enough, after all.
But it had some of that feeling to it. There was that same
sense of seeing, suddenly, a completely different standard
by which to measure myself, of becoming aware of the
extent to which I make a life by stringing together one
pleasure after the next—golf, travel, good meals, lovemaking and thoughts of lovemaking, my new car, my nice
house, my happy family. It's natural enough, I suppose. I
don't suppose a life like that earns one a reservation

among the damned. It's just that, for those few hours in Parolise, I felt myself to be in the presence of a deeper, truer goodness, and felt the little welter of shame it raises, then the defensiveness, the justifications, the instinct for finding something not so good in the lives of those two women, to ease the comparison. The instinct of the cynic.

I have never quite been able to make myself believe in the existence of the devil. In spite of the horror of torture and rape, of war and abuse, it has never seemed quite possible to me that a vicious spirit roams the human world, drawing souls toward eternal fire. Buddhists believe we each live thousands of lifetimes, paying to the last drop for the harm we do each other, growing very gradually purer and better until we cast off our illusions of an individual identity and merge with some larger spirit. Perhaps that is the way everything has been arranged, I do not know.

What I do know—or at least what I believe—is that there are various responses to the predicament we find ourselves in: from Stalin to Gandhi and a billion variations between. At one end are the selfish and the cruel, and at the other, the generous and humble; and in the large middle territory, the unimaginably complicated mixture that is the rest of us. It seems to me on most days that the individual soul is, in fact, home to every potentiality at once, that I contain the torturer and the saint, and so do you. In some lives—Hitler's, Idi Amin's—the instinct for violence plays itself out on a massive scale; in others, the identical impulse has less opportunity, but we indulge it in much the same way, reaching for divisiveness when we might just as easily reach for union, hurting when we might try to heal, wanting to eliminate or defame the Other, whether that other is black or white or woman, Jew or homosexual, rich or poor, Palestinian, Protestant, Catholic, saved or damned.

By some spiritual will or ethereal magic, the one we call "good" manages, hour by hour, to set the selfish, divisive impulse aside and behave as if the other person is herself. In some mystical traditions, there is even the notion that such a purified soul actually becomes God. The idea seems impossibly distant to me, but I suspect Michelangelo may have understood it. Perhaps the faces of the saved as he painted them on the ceiling of the Sistine Chapel wore such expressions of awe and timidity because they were not yet quite ready to believe in the abundance of their own potential goodness, in the generosity and power they saw reflected in the face of their God. Maybe, in that moment, in the presence of that enormous selfless force, some devilish voice still whispered in their ears: No. It cannot be. It is not possible.

The Notion of North

One January day, standing on a cross-country ski trail in the southern Adirondacks, two friends and I discovered we shared a fantasy. We each harbored a dream of driving north into the Canadian wilderness as far as the road would take us.

The three of us are what used to be called "family men." We have all been married for more than fifteen years, and we say good things about our wives behind their backs. We are all fathers of one child—daughters born relatively late in our lives—whom we dote on. We work on our houses and yards, we change diapers, we don't drink very much, or gamble very much, or fail to call when we're late coming home. We are, in short, ordinary, decent, domestic men, married to good women, living out a kind of modest American dream on beautiful pieces of New England acreage.

And for years now, separately and secretly, we have imagined getting in the car and driving away from that dream, north, into some of the least tame territory on the continent. Not forever. Not in anger or frustration or in search of another woman. Not on foot or by dogsled or in a hot-air balloon. Just north, in a car, for a week or so.

Why?

I will not try to answer that question for my friends Dean and Peter, for men in general, or even for all fathers and longtime husbands. And I will certainly not try to speak for women—married to me or otherwise. But I do not believe I am alone in saying this: For many of us, within the symphony of communal life, there is a note of solitude or wildness that must be struck from time to time in order for a certain harmony to be maintained. This note may be as mundane as an hour alone gardening or woodworking, or as daring as a sail across the Atlantic. Or, between those extremes, a solitary drive north into the Canadian forests.

Tuesday evening almost always finds me at peace in the bosom of domestic life. I feed our daughter, change her into her sleeping clothes, and hand her over to Amanda, who puts her to bed.

But wife and daughter were away on this particular Tuesday, gone to comfort Amanda's mother, who had, three weeks earlier, lost her husband of fifty years. It had been a sudden death, instant exchange of presence for absence, personality for mystery, companionship for loneliness, and the whole family was struggling to come to terms with it.

So this Tuesday found me driving north from my weekly golf match, instead of home to help with the domestic duties. North, I hoped, toward a clearer appreciation of a certain fragility and beauty that is too often blurred by routine.

In contrast to the aborigines with their walkabouts, our society, so fast-paced, sophisticated, and focused on the material side of things, does not have any tradition of solitary getaways. There is no time for such indulgences. (A friend of mine contends that the image that best captures our era is this: his wife standing in front of the microwave as the seconds count down, stamping her foot and shouting at the winking plastic face, "Come on, dammit!") The great economic machine to which we are strapped, ankle and wrist, and which gives us, in return, the greatest sense of comfort and security in the history of our species, sees nothing productive or admirable about a workless week alone. In fact, solitude is wholly suspect in American culture, the province of assassins, child molesters, and unwashed mountain-man eccentrics.

And so, as one sets off along the highway listening to John Hiatt singing "Something Wild," one cannot help but spend a moment fingering the thin lining of guilt in the billowing coat of freedom.

There was a small chip of moon on that Tuesday night, tumbling slow motion through a prematurely autumnal sky. Hurricane Bonnie was aimed at the outer banks. The ruble was sinking like a can of caviar in a bathtub. The Clintons were on the Vineyard, sorting out their own domestic scene, trapped in a dream-life where solitude and wildness are out of the question.

And the right side of Route 91 went north, away from headlines and scandal, away from the lawn and the telephone and the comfort of friendship. North.

I made it only as far as White River Junction, Vermont, on that first night, and slept in a neutered and pleasant chain motel. There, the imagined journey took shape: a fantasy landscape, fantasy conversations, fantasy meals. Bear, moose, cold northern skies. An exotic driveabout of the first order.

The actual trip, of course, refused to fit itself into such a neat pattern. This guaranteed disappointment is as much a part of traveling as sandtraps are a part of golf. On the night before a game, who forms a pleasant mental image of hitting into a sandtrap?

And, on the first night of a trip, who imagines being detained at the Canadian border the next day by a dominatrix/customs agent who punches in your license plate and then asks—four times—if you've ever gone before a judge? Then keeps you waiting twenty minutes without saying why. Then sends a colleague out who asks you the same question again, and who eventually reveals the secret information that you have something called "a Vermont I.D. number," which turns out to be the result of a fishing-without-a-license fine on Lake Dunmore—all paid up, thank you—from 1983.

What optimistic traveler would ever envision a motel not far from the shores of the St. Lawrence, thirty miles south of Quebec City, with a room stinking so thoroughly of disinfectant that you have to leave the door open for fifteen minutes before moving in? Where you think the shower in the next room sounds like a freight train . . . until the real CN freight goes by, a hundred feet beyond the patched and shaking wall.

Or, on the positive side: who could imagine the next

morning's ham and onion omelet cooked to order by a Chinese immigrant who speaks solid enough English to direct you to the nearest golf course? Or the golf game there with two men and a woman, retired Quebecois, one of whom—a trim, quiet father of a daughter—tells you, at the end of the match, in heavily accented but precise English, "You are a good man."

This, then, was turning out to be not the imagined trip but the actual, at once better and worse. Driving, eating, getting lost, scrambling through dusty mental precincts in search of a long-ago forgotten French vocabulary. But the actual trip, after two nights on the road, had too tame a texture to it. Tee times and music tapes, herds of Guernseys on hillsides and steep metal roofs painted in primary colors: nice enough, but what could such things show me about my life at home?

It is interesting to consider where we turn for a perspective on how we live. Rabbis, priests, ministers, gurus. Our spouse, our friends, our therapist, our favorite daytime talk show. We do not suffer from a shortage of counsel. What we suffer from, I think, besides a lack of time, is the almost complete absence of any cultural emphasis on the interior life. To make matters worse, the loudest voices decrying that absence—I am thinking of certain TV preachers and professional moralists—sound so judgmental and narrow-minded that they turn the earnest search for meaning into a circus of catchphrases, bigotry, and quickly cashed checks.

The Koran counsels that "the light is in houses" of "people who are not diverted by business or commerce from remembrance of God." But the problem, in these times, is that the line between commerce and religious devotion has been blurred—from both sides. Our houses of worship have impressive stock portfolios, and we hire our greatest architects and builders to make corporate headquarters, not cathedrals. We do not work day and night for peace of mind, we work day and night for a piece of the rock.

Which is what I was trying to drive away from. Not just accounts payable and receivable, but the entire network of errands, details, social obligations, e-mail, junk mail, voice mail, oil changes, cartridge changes, software changes, lists of lists of lists of what absolutely had to be done. I wanted, like a pressed field commander, to find some high ground from which to survey the battle.

The high ground came into view just beyond Quebec City. After ten minutes or so of Interstate madness, the capital's bland suburbs gave way, very suddenly, to something greener. It was as if I'd crossed an invisible border between frenzy and emptiness.

The road climbed and dipped through an unpeopled landscape, two-thousand-foot hills rolling off into the blue distance. There seemed to be a different lake every few kilometers, their inky surfaces reflecting silent Canadian forests and a parade of August clouds. Warnings to Brake for Moose, dense endless stands of fir and maple, sandy barrens festooned with patches of lichen. Not a house, not a boat, nothing but two lanes of asphalt that lay empty for minutes at a time, and thousands of square miles of uninhabited woods. My notion of north, exactly.

Strange then, and extremely disappointing, that this strip of tar should deposit the untamed traveler, after three hours, on the shore of Lac St. Jean, an enormous body of fresh water surrounded by sleepy and completely domesticated farming towns like Roberval and St. Felicien. That night I telephoned Amanda from another dimly lit motel room.

"This is due north from our house," I said, "as far as the road goes. And it's about as wild as Lake Winnipesaukee."

"Can't you go farther?"

"Only if you turn northwest. There's a town there called Chibougamau. But it would add another day to the trip, at least."

"What did you say the town is called?"

"Chibougamau."

"You have to go," she said. "Just based on the name alone, you have to."

So I went.

After curling along the lake for fifteen miles, the road branched off to the northwest. More ragged and less commercial there, it ran past farmhouses with scrawny stands of corn and statues of Mary in the yard, the Quebec flag flying here and there like a favorite shirt on display. There was less variety to the trees—stunted fir with the very occasional white birch—and the sky had a paler cast. Against that background I saw the kind of sign I had been looking for: "Next Gas 190 km." Why did the sight of it make me so happy?

Along the two-lane tar road to Chibougamau (pronounced: She-Boo-gah-moo) the trees and hills were noticeably smaller, as if rendered permanently humble by centuries of, cold and snow. Traffic consisted of logging trucks rocketing past in the opposite direction, and four-wheel-drive pickups pushing eighty. No rest stops, no truck lanes, no police cars. Nothing but trees and lakes and long views into the taiga, and every twenty miles or so, a phone booth with a red SOS sign beside it.

I'd taken two hitchhikers out of a downpour near Quebec City, and one of them had said, of Chibougamau, "You're liable to see Indians walking bears on leashes along the main drag."

But that, it turned out, was a twenty-year-old's hyperbole. I did see a very young boy strutting along the sidewalk there on Friday night smoking a cigarette; and a fellow urinating in an alley not as far as he might have gone from the eyes of passing pedestrians; and, in a not so nice bar up the road, I did notice a young woman lead a young man away from one of the tables, into an area set off by bead curtains, where they lay down more or less out of sight for ten minutes and separately re-emerged.

In fact, though, Chibougamau turned out to be an appealing place, a few blocks of modest houses surrounding a one-street commercial district with music playing from speakers on the light poles and a frontier feel to it. The most exotic thing I came across was a sign in a clothing store saying "Thank you for shopping with us," in French, English, and Cree.

Saturday was windy and overcast, sixty-five degrees. In the afternoon, suffering from road weariness and wondering at the foolishness of the whole adventure, I drove to the town beach, ignored all the BEACH CLOSED signs, and took a quick swim there, alone, shivering, staring north in waist-deep water like a pilgrim looking for his elusive God.

I dried off on the windy beach and felt that the cords that bound me had been stretched to breaking. I could keep going now, I saw that—farther and farther away from anything safe, and known, and pretending to promise a future. Clearly, it was time to turn back. I returned to my respectable hotel and had fresh trout for dinner, and the next morning set off on the 750-mile drive home.

My driveabout was obviously not the equivalent of forty days in the desert, or a solitary ascent of K-2. I am neither holy nor heroic. But that is exactly the point: for the ordinary man or woman, what is it that the cluttered life hides, and how does one go about revealing it?

Being away alone for a week did not magically sweep away my little neuroses and insecurities, the quirks, urges, and subtle greed that keep me at some distance from what the Zen masters call "one's true face."

What it did was cast all that into sharper relief, so that, upon rejoining the race, I might make some effort to change those things, if I want to, if I can. And in changing them, see a little less darkly through the glass. And in seeing more clearly through the glass, understand what my mother-in-law feels so poignantly now in her pain: what it means to have another life there close against your own, what it really means.

How A Soul Is Fashioned

A five-dollar palm reader in Washington, D.C., once told me I'd be rich and famous and do a lot of traveling, and would die at the age of eighty-four. She had the traveling part right, at least. And if the eighty-four prediction turns out to hit the mark, as well, then she will have managed to be correct in her predictions 50 percent of the time, an average most of us would settle for.

I am forty-seven now, deep into the territory of middle age. Married twenty-one years to the same good woman, father of a beautiful girl, with another child on the way— making up for lost time, as a friend said to me on the telephone last night. Though I occasionally suffer from the kind of crisis said to afflict men and women at this stage of life—a vague dissatisfaction with myself and with the whole sad architecture of human existence—it's almost clear to me in better moments that the show has a design to it. Perhaps that design rests, as Hindus and Buddhists believe, on the notion that the soul lives innumerable lifetimes in different bodies and different places until it prefects itself and merges with the Almighty. The idea goes a long way toward explaining some of life's thornier inequities. But even if that isn't true, even if all we get is our twenty, sixty, or eighty-four years, it seems probable to me that the process is an educational one, a kind of training. What we are being trained for I haven't the slightest idea. But, like most educational experiences, this one, at its best, seems to follow an arc from the hubris of ignorance, through the trials and exhilarations of apprenticeship, and into a mastery that's made up of a nice blend of confidence and humility. That's similar to the trajectory of a good love relationship, isn't it? Don't we fall in love under the spell of a kind of blissful, sensual conceit, convinced of the goodness and attractiveness of ourselves and our beloved, sure that nothing but pleasure lies ahead? And don't most people then sink—sometimes slowly, sometimes quickly—into a swamp of conflict and dissatisfaction, two souls rubbing hard against each other as they slog along, all the differences apparent now, most of the shine of infatuation gone dull? Sometimes love drowns there in that muck. Sometimes the lovers just get stranded, waist-deep in complaint, half-ignoring each other or sniping at each other across a short distance for fifty years. And sometimes, with a bit of luck or grace and a good amount of effort, they manage to struggle through and make it as far as dry land again, and walk on together, muddied and bruised, but linked in a deeper way.

But that's too simple an image to contain the complexity of love. Even in the deepest part of the swamp there is usually a flower or two. And even the strong bonds of longtime affection are frayed and cracked by some version or another of what the courts call "irreconcilable differences." There are always irreconcilable differences, always this frustrating separateness, one from the other, always a stubborn opinion, desire, or quirk that flecks the pure fabric of unity. But in relationships that thrive, in lives that succeed, there is always, it seems to me, a movement toward humility. If we are lucky enough to live lives protected from the worst forms of degradation and protracted agony, then humility is the major subject of our earthly academic career, the piece of music we must learn to play.

I was born to parents who had great ambitions for me. Who among us can say otherwise? There may be something particularly intense about the ambition of first-generation Americans, though: partly to give them a richer, better life, their own parents had made the great leap from a poorer or more troubled country to this one. So much was expected of these first generation Americans and yet they were born here with no tradition of local success behind them, no connection to the power elite, no wealth or property that had been passed to their families down the generations. My father and mother were bright, strong, hardworking, and they made a good life for themselves and for us, but there was always a ceiling over their heads, a certain downward-working pressure, an economic and cultural establishment and an entrenched social system that let them scramble a notch or two up the ladder, but no further. My mother was the daughter of a factory foreman and wanted to be a doctor, but she settled for physical therapy. My father's longed-for law degree came only when he turned sixty. Both of them settled for a string of used cars, a five-day motel vacation once every other year, and nice clothes bought on sale.

Neither of them ever complained very loudly about the material facts of their lives, as if aware not only of what hovered above them, but what lay below. After all, we had plenty to eat, a nice house, friends, health, faith enough to carry us through the hard times. But all around them, just beyond the borders of their situation, my parents could see evidence of a better life, or at least what seemed to be a better life: newer cars, larger yards, quieter neighborhoods, people who owned second homes, whose children went to prestigious colleges and moved from those idyllic campuses into successful and lucrative careers. When I came along, on a cloudless September afternoon in 1953 (they were thirty-seven and thirty-one, my father had the death of a wife and child behind him, my mother had suffered the first of several miscarriages, they were living in four small rooms above my father's parents), the occasion was greeted with a great deal of joy and gratitude. At the same time, probably without their knowing it, an enormous cargo of ambition was shifted onto my small shoulders.

When a few years went by and I turned out to be "smart" as we used to say—meaning I had the kind of mental agility over which so much fuss is made in this society: I could learn words and add numbers quickly—that ambition began to be molded into a clearer shape. At a very early age I remember telling people I wanted to be a doctor when I grew up. I didn't know the slightest thing about how doctors actually lived; I had gotten the idea from my parents, because, to them, being a doctor meant breaking through the ceiling that held them down; it meant crashing out of the working class and into the quiet life of stock portfolios and automatic respect. Age eight and I was a doctor-in-waiting, fawned over by teachers, praised by uncles and aunts, walking down Essex Street from Barrows School with a gold star on the middle of my forehead. How could I have known about humility then? And what would it have been worth, in any case, next to the ten-dollar bill my uncle Cammy used to give me for getting all A's? To make matters worse, or at least more complicated, I was good at sports, too: the fastest runner in the school until Michael Sokolowski came along in fourth grade; an all-star shortstop in Little League; a better streetfighter, at least in the very early going, than my Essex Street friends Frankie Imbrescia and Albert Santosuosso. Street hockey, basketball, skating, touch football – everything except swimming came naturally and easily to me in those early years, though it was hardly due to any effort of my own. Like my two athletic brothers, I'd inherited good genes, that was all: Uncle Cammy had been a baseball star, his son Joe a pro prospect until his career was cut short by an auto accident; my mother's father had pitched semi-pro ball into his fifties, and she herself had been the city tennis champion, and played softball, as a high school senior, with the women who would later be featured in *A League of Their Own*.

On top of all this, I was the product of two families –

the Haydocks and the Merullos – who were a little bit like royalty in their respective parts of the city. My mother's father was Boss to most of the men on Olive Street, respected and liked, and had owned a car before any of his neighbors; and my father's father had been a boss at one time, too, had also been one of the first people in Revere with an automobile, and now presided, with an Old World dignity, over a brood of eight children, their spouses and kids, all of whom came to his house every Sunday. Grandma Haydock was famous for her beauty, and for being able to recite poetry, from memory, by the hour. Grandma Merullo was thought to be a holy woman, and the best cook this side of Naples. Every time my brothers and I visited their houses, it would be a festival of embraces and praise, gifts, food, a warm sense of belonging. Everywhere in the city we were known by our connection to respected older relatives – "I'm a friend of your aunt," people would say, "I went to school with your cousin," "I played ball with your grandfather," and it was always said as if these people felt proud and lucky to have known us. How wonderful it all was, how sweet. I was a Merullo, I was from Revere, I was good on the diamond and good in the classroom, I was going to be a doctor.

That was the beginning. In the years between then and now – thank God, thank life – so much of that proud edifice has been dismantled. First, in junior high school, my meager abilities as a streetfighter abandoned me: I was beaten up a couple of times, embarrassed, humiliated. Then, in high school, I met people who were so much smarter than I, and in such a deeper sense. Not a lot more time passed before I began to understand that owning a car in Revere, Massachusetts, even in the 1940s, really wasn't quite a sign of royalty after all, that the Catholic Church might not be the only refuge of the chosen ones, that there are some Italians who were obnoxious and crude, that becoming a doctor was one of the last things on earth I wanted. In my twenties I broke my upper back, in my thirties I had surgery to remove a disc from my lower back, and in my early forties it turned out that I'd inherited something called psoriatic arthritis, all of which added up to decades of daily pain and weekly muscle spasms, tens of thousands of dollars in chiropractor bills. I took medication for the pain, which skewed my digestion, which affected my sleep, and so on. There was some very rough sledding between Amanda and me in the early and middle years, the sudden passing of my father, persistent financial worries, a long string of rejections before my first book came out.

Doesn't everyone have woes along these same lines—a chronic sleep problem, an enormous and shattering business failure, an auto accident, estrangement, divorce, disability, depression, disinterest? I'm steering clear of the very worst cases here—victims of torture, children born with the HIV virus or suffering from cancer, men and women driven insane by grief or abuse. But don't even the sweetest-looking lives hold pockets of pain in them?

The point of all that striving and suffering—if it has a point—is a matter of individual opinion. Each of us forms an explanation for the existence of failure and pain in our lives, and every explanation is a mini-religion all its own.

My religion, I suppose, the belief system I've made for myself to render the events of my life meaningful, is this: in a mysterious fashion not completely understandable to us, everything moves the individual soul toward humility.

Which is not to say I am humble. Old habits die hard, and there is a way in which the conceits of youth mutate into other forms: one can be proud of being humble, even of trying to be humble, even of thinking or writing about such things as trying to be humble; one can think one knows, when in fact one doesn't. Still, speaking with my secret self, I find it hard to argue against one idea: that, in most lives, the rough hand of time sands the soul smooth. Time shrinks the ego—even if the most egotistical among us must wait until old age, or the very moment of death, for that to happen. The arc of a well-lived life, a life in which good fortune is accepted gratefully and bad fortune borne without too much bitterness, leads toward a kind of interior smallness, the very opposite, perhaps, of what I used to feel walking down Essex Street with a star on my forehead. It seems to me that this is the real meaning behind St. Paul's "It is no longer I who lives but God who lives within me," and the Hebrew scholar Martin Buber's idea of an I-Thou relationship in which we see the other as the self, and even the often-misinterpreted Buddhist notion of "emptiness." It is a kind of smallness they are all talking about, a way of still being around without taking up quite so much space.

If the ego is small enough, and the will is put to good use, then life sands the soul smooth—that's the notion that carries me. From that small, smooth perspective, belief in some kind of divine force is not so much a matter of faith as of observation; the miracle of things is clearly apparent: the movement of a child's eyelid, the wide swing of the planets. It is the I itself, the enormous, demanding, petulant, perpetually dissatisfied "I" that hangs like a bolt of gauze between the face of the soul and the world's wonder. Little by little, lifetime by lifetime perhaps, the curtain thins, there's no stopping it. You break your back, you work in Russia, you fail in something that matters to you, you find love, lose it, find it again, bring up children (what could possibly be more humbling?) and set them off on the same path; you follow the line of your own particular fate, a fate built partly of your soul's unique essence, and partly of your class and place and time. You march along through the mud and past the flowers, toward, in the end of ends, as the Russians say, a small small godliness of your own making.

Acknowledgements

First, thanks to Amanda for her love and unwavering support. I am grateful also to Cynthia Cannell for, among other things, introducing me to Deanne Urmy, to Deanne for her enthusiasm and advice, to Robert Hemenway for his careful suggestions, to my friends Peter Grudin and Blair Orfall for taking the time to read parts of this book and offer wise counsel, and to Helene Atwan and all the people at Beacon Press, with whom it was such a pleasure to work on the first edition. And, to Peter Sarno, another Revere kid, for his generosity and kind determination to keep this book alive.

CPSIA information can be obtained at www.ICGtesting.com
Printed in the USA
BVOW030839270911

272235BV00001B/103/P